THE DEVELOPMENT OF
THE DRAMA

THE DEVELOPMENT OF
THE DRAMA

BY
BRANDER MATTHEWS

BOOKS FOR LIBRARIES PRESS
FREEPORT, NEW YORK

First Published 1903
Reprinted 1972

INTERNATIONAL STANDARD BOOK NUMBER:
0-8369-6801-8

LIBRARY OF CONGRESS CATALOG CARD NUMBER:
79-39199

PRINTED IN THE UNITED STATES OF AMERICA
BY
NEW WORLD BOOK MANUFACTURING CO., INC.
HALLANDALE, FLORIDA 33009

PREFACE

THE interesting story of the slow evolution of the drama, from its rude beginnings far back in the forgotten past to the pictorial complexity of the present day, has not hitherto been told in a single volume. Most of the existing histories of dramatic literature are unduly distended with critical biographies of distinguished playwrights. Some of them—in particular, Schlegel's—are filled with the echoes of bygone controversies. No one of them, moreover, has taken into account the threefold influence exerted on the form of the drama of every epoch by the demands of the actors, by the size and shape and circumstances of the theaters of that time, and by the changing prejudices of the contemporary audiences.

Each of these influences has been kept in mind constantly in the present attempt clearly to trace the development of the drama itself, down through the ages, without ever delaying to narrate the lives of the leading writers who found in this form of literary art their chief means of self-expression. Such criticism as there may be in the following pages is not so much philosophical or even esthetic as it is technical; it is concerned less with the poetry which illumines the master-pieces of the great dramatists than it is with the sheer craftsmanship of the most skilful play-wrights. The desire of the author has been to bring out the essential unity of the history of the drama and to make plain the permanence of the principles underlying the art of the stage.

As it has seemed best to leave the book unen-cumbered with foot-notes, it may be recorded here that the conventions of the drama have been con-sidered (at greater length than was here possible) in a paper published in a volume entitled 'The Historical Novel, and Other Essays'— a volume which also contains an essay on 'The Relation of the Drama to Literature.' In the third edition of another volume, 'Aspects of Fiction,' there was included a paper on 'The Importance of the Folk-Theater.'

Of the ten lectures which make up the present volume, one or more have been delivered during the past two or three years at the Royal Institution of Great Britain, at the Brooklyn Institute, at Columbia University, and before the National Institute of Arts and Letters.

B. M.

Columbia University
in the City of New York.

CONTENTS

I. THE ART OF THE DRAMATIST

I

CRITICISM nowadays is franker than ever before in acknowledging the kinship of the various arts—painting and sculpture, music and poetry and the drama. As an American poet once made an Italian painter say,

> It seems to me
> All arts are one,—all branches on one tree,—
> All fingers, as it were, upon one hand.

And yet at the same time criticism is ever revealing an increasing appreciation of the special characteristics of each of the arts, a keener relish for the qualities peculiar to that art alone and absent from all the others. While every art can make us see and feel and think, each in its own way, the means of each are as different as may be; and whenever their methods are confused there is at once loss of power and misdirection of energy. It is a part of the duty of the epic poet to tell us a story; of the painter to give us an impression of the visible world; of the sculptor to fill our eyes with the beauty of form alone; and of the musician to charm our ears with rhythm and with harmony. But when the painter puts his chief reliance upon story-telling, and when the poet seeks to rival the musician, then of a certainty will they fail to attain the higher summits of possible achievement in their own arts.

It is in their technical processes that the arts are strangers, in the methods by which the artist expresses himself; and this is why technic is again coming into the high esteem in which it was held during the Renascence, the most glorious epoch for all the allied arts since the day when Pericles ceased to rule over Athens. Craftsmanship, the mastery of his tools—this is what we are now demanding of the practitioner of every art. Craftsmanship can be his for the asking; he can have it if he will pay the price in toil and care and time. The message he may have to deliver is the gift of God, after all; but the artist himself is responsible for the clearness and the eloquence of its delivery. The prime duty of the craftsman is to know his trade, that he may give a fitting form to whatsoever ideas may hereafter possess him. His second obligation is to understand the possibilities of his art, its limitations, its boundaries, so that he may conquer all temptation to try to do what cannot be done by the only means at his command.

One art there is, and only one, which can avail itself at will of almost every device of all the other arts. One art there is which can reach out and borrow the aid of the poet, the painter, the sculptor, the musician, compelling them all to help it toward its own perfection. One art there is which, without danger of confusion, without departing from its own object, without loss of force, can, at one and the same time, tell a story, and give an impression of the visible world, and fill our eyes with the beauty of form, and charm our ears with rhythm and with harmony. This one art is the art of the drama, the art which most completely displays the life of man—"the youngest of the sister arts," the British poet called it, "where all their beauty blends";

> For ill can Poetry express
>   Full many a tone of thought sublime,
> And Painting, mute and motionless,
>   Steals but a glance of time.
> But by the mighty actor brought,
>   Illusion's perfect triumphs come;
> Verse ceases to be airy thought,
>   And Sculpture to be dumb.

To many of us the drama gives merely unthinking amusement in the playhouse; and to not a few others it presents itself as the loftiest form of poetry. To some its chief quality is that it enables them to disentangle the philosophy of the dramatist himself, and to declare his ethical code; and to others it affords satisfaction because it is ever a gallery of character-portraits, wherein we can each of us enlarge our knowledge of our fellow-man. To a few it is significant as the material by which we can best distinguish national characteristics; and to more it is of value chiefly because of its words, which can be scanned and parsed and traced to their sources. And to the scantiest group of all, perhaps, dramatic literature is ever interesting because it is the highest manifestation of the dramatic instinct universal in mankind, and because it supplies abundantly the special pleasure which only the art of the dramatist can provide.

To this smallest body I confess myself to belong. The drama is interesting in many ways, no doubt; but to me, I admit, it is always most interesting when it is considered simply as drama —as a work of dramaturgic craftsmanship prepared especially to be performed by actors, in a theater, before an audience. As all the great plays were written to be played, it is perhaps most profitable always to consider them from this point of view—from the point of view of the playhouse, in the terms of which they were conceived. Other methods of approach there are

4

also, of course, but this is ever the most necessary. Nor is it a work of supererogation to
repeat this apparently obvious statement, and to
persist in reiterating it, since the essential quality
of the mighty masterpieces of dramatic literature
is only too frequently neglected. Praise is abundant for the poetry that adorns the great plays,
for their sentences of pregnant wisdom, for the
subtlety of their authors' insight into conflicting
human motives; but due consideration is seldom
bestowed on the skill with which the action is
conducted—the action, which is the heart of the
play, and without which it is lifeless and inert.

To some of us it seems like an arrant absurdity
that school-boys should now be forced to scan
the pathetic passages of Sophocles, and that
school-girls should be set to parse the swift re-
partees of Shakspere, before these young students
have been made to see clearly that the tragedies
of the Greek and the romantic-comedies of the
Englishman are as great as they are, not because
of any mere metrical or grammatical felicity, but
because of their admirable dramaturgic structure
—because Sophocles and Shakspere were both of
them born playwrights; because they were, first
of all, not writers of poetry, but makers of plays,
masters of all the tricks of their trade, and possessing completely all the resources of their craft.
The dramatist needs to have his full share of play-

5

making skill before he can adequately display his power as a poet; and it is this play-making skill, this dramaturgic faculty, which sustains and vitalizes every masterpiece of dramatic literature.

The dramaturgic faculty is evolved slowly with the growth of civilization; and play-making skill is one of the latest of human accomplishments. But the rudimentary effort is everywhere visible, even among the most primitive peoples. As we consider the history of human progress we perceive that the drama is almost the very earliest of the arts, as early, perhaps, as the art of personal adornment; and we discover, also, that it is the very latest to attain its complete expression. Only among the races which may be exceptionally endowed with energy of imagination and with power of construction does the drama arrive at its highest possibility of achievement. In these rare cases it is the most splendid expression of the special gifts of these races; it is the sublime summit of their literatures. But in the noblest works of the great Greek dramatists, and in the most powerful plays of the Elizabethans, the same principles are applied which we discover doubtfully in the rudest theatrical attempts of the lowest savages. Sophocles profited by Aeschylus, and Shakspere by Marlowe; but if it had not been for many humble beginners following one another, each bettering the effort of him who went

6

before, and all alike forgotten now, Aeschylus
and Marlowe would never have found a form of
drama ready to their hands.   By considering the
dramaturgic art throughout its whole history,
we can best win our way to an understanding
of its essential principles.   We learn most, no
doubt, by a study of the workmanship of the
undisputed masters; and yet only at our peril do
we neglect the obscure origins of the art far back
in the remotest past.

II

It is out of crude efforts, such as may still be
observed among the Eskimo and the tribes of the
Amazon, that the dramatic art was toilfully developed by our own predecessors as taste refined and
civilization advanced.   The traditions of these
rude play-makers were passed down from generation to generation, and the art slowly discovered
itself.   The true dramatist is like the true states-
man in recognizing that nothing substantial can
be made out of hand, and that nothing survives
which is not a development of institutions already
existing.   The one untried novelty in the Consti-
tution of the United States soon failed of its purpose; and whenever the merely literary critics
have succeeded in persuading the dramatic poet
to discard the playhouse methods of his own
day, the result has been disastrous.   Art must

always make haste slowly; and no art ever sprang like Minerva full grown from the head of Jove—not even the dramatic art in the city of the violet crown, where Phidias wrought the towering statue of the wise goddess.

In these earlier attempts at the drama there is no tincture of literature; and more often than not these primitive plays were even unwritten, being wrought out by word of mouth. Sometimes they were a combination of pantomimic action with song and dance; and sometimes the dramatic element served solely to emphasize the important passages of a narrative chant. In the childhood of a race or of an individual, we discover that the lyric, the dramatic, and the narrative are only imperfectly differentiated from one another; and we can gain some insight into primitive conditions of the drama by going back to our own childhood, since youth is the special season of make-believe, strong as that instinct is in all the seven ages of man. The child is ever imitative and mimetic. The little girl is willing to credit her doll with feelings like her own and to hold converse with it; she is glad to pretend that it is ill; and she is delighted to be able to change the sheets on its bed as the trained nurse changed hers when she herself lay sick. One of the most striking discoveries of modern science has made it plain that we must each of us follow the development of our ancestors, and pass through the successive stages of animal and social evolution. Much of this journey takes place before we are born, but not a little is left for the years of infancy and of youth.

It is from the observation of children and from the study of savages that the comparative anthropologist has been able to throw so much light on the earlier stages of human progress. Professor Grosse, in his illuminating discussion of the 'Beginnings of Art,' points out that pure narrative "requires a command of language and of one's own body which is rarely found," and that "children and primitive peoples likewise are indeed unable to make any narration without accompanying it with the appropriate demeanor and play of gesture." Professor Grosse notes that common usage means by a drama, "not the relation of an event enlivened by mimicry, but its direct mimic and verbal representation by several persons"; and he asserts the existence of this in even the lowest stages of culture. He recognizes as one root of a more elaborate drama the duet of the Greenlanders, for example, in which "the two singers are not only relating their adventure, but are representing it by mimic gestures"; and he finds a second source in the mimic dance. Out of one or the other a true drama gets itself evolved at last; and its slow rise in the dramatic scale is in strict proportion to the rise of the people itself in the scale of civilization. The form is enlarged and enriched; it expands in various directions; it will lack literature for long years, until at last there arrives a dramatic poet who takes the form as he finds it, with all its imperfections and inconsistencies. He accepts it without hesitation, certain that it will serve his purpose, since it has already proved that it is satisfactory to the contemporaries whom he has to please. In time, after he has mastered the form as he has received it from his predecessors, he makes it his own and remodels it to his increasing needs, when he has gained confidence in himself, and when he has broadened his outlook on life.

As simple as any primitive play, and as characteristic, is this pantomime represented by the Aleutian Islanders: " An Aleut, who was armed with a bow, represented a hunter, another a bird. The former expressed by gestures how very glad he was he had found so fine a bird; nevertheless he would not kill it. The other imitated the motions of a bird seeking to escape the hunter. He at last, after a long delay, pulled his bow and shot: the bird reeled, fell, and died. The hunter danced for joy; but finally he became troubled, repented having killed so fine a bird, and lamented it. Suddenly the dead bird rose, turned into a beautiful woman, and fell into the hunter's arms." Here we have a dramatic action, complete in itself, and yet extremely simple. It was capable of being performed anywhere and anywhen, since it called for no costumes, no scenery, and no stage-properties. It needed no words to be plainly understood. It dealt with elementary emotions, following one another in obvious succession. It was wholly within the comprehension of the spectators; and by the magical resuscitation and transformation at the end, it was likely to appeal to the love of the marvelous always potent among savages.

Dropping down from Alaska to Australia, we find a more spectacular pantomime, requiring more performers and a more careful preparation, even if not an actual rehearsal. On a moonlight night some five hundred spectators gathered in a clearing of the woods lighted by a huge fire; and on one side there was seated an orchestra of about a hundred women. "The first scene consisted in the representation of a herd of cattle which came out of the woods to pasture on the meadow. The black players had painted themselves appropriately to their characters. The imitation was skilful; the motion and behavior of each head of the herd were amusingly natural. Some lay on the ground and chewed their cuds. Others stood and scratched themselves with their horns and hind feet, or licked their companions or their calves. Others rubbed one another's heads in a friendly way. After their bucolic idyl had lasted a little while, the second scene began. A band of blacks were perceived creeping upon the herd, with all the precautions which the natives use in such cases. At length they were near enough, and two cattle fell, struck by spears, to the highest delight of the spectators, who broke out in enthusiastic applause. The hunters began to skin their prey, dress it, and cut it up—all with the most painstaking exactness. The third scene was opened with a trotting of horses in the wood. Immediately afterward a troop of white men appeared on horseback. Their faces were painted a whitish brown; their bodies blue or red, to represent colored shirts; and the lower parts of their legs, in the absence of gaiters, were wrapped with brushwood. These white men galloped straight up to the blacks, fired, and drove them back. The latter collected again, and a desperate battle began, in which the blacks beat the whites and drove them back. The whites bit off their cartridges, fixed the caps on their guns—in short, went regularly through all the motions of loading and firing. As often as a black fell the spectators groaned, but when a white man bit the dust a loud shout of joy went up. At last the whites were disgracefully put to flight, to the unbounded delight of the natives, who were so excited that the merest trifle might have changed the sham fight into bloody earnest."

There we have a sophisticated analog of one of the best known of American spectacles—the attack on the Deadwood coach and the driving off of the Sioux by Buffalo Bill, aided by his reckless rough-riders. In one peculiarity the Australian pantomime is more significant than the Aleutian: we are told that one of the performers took no actual part, but served as the director of the whole exhibition, accompanying the successive scenes of the pantomime with an explanatory song. Here we catch a glimpse of the expositor, who in the medieval drama was expected to comment upon the successive scenes of a passion-play and to expound their meaning.

Perhaps there is no need now to point out again the absence of any literary quality from these plays of the Aleutians and of the Australians, or from those of all savages in a similar stage of social development. In fact, pantomime itself is proof positive that the drama can be absolutely independent of literature, that it can come into being without the aid of the written word, and that it can support itself by its own devices. In the earliest periods of culture the drama does exist without literature; and it is only when the people among which it is cherished reaches a very high state of civilization that the drama is able to appear as the loftiest form of poetry, after having lived for centuries, perhaps, without any literary pretensions whatever.

These inherent tendencies do not cease to be effective with the advent of civilization; if they are truly inherent in humanity they must be at work to-day. And altho the action of these instinctive forces is not now with us what it was when our remote ancestors were yet uncivilized, still it is visible if only we take the trouble to look for it. There are few periods when the spontaneous growth of the unliterary drama is not to be seen somewhere; and the history of the theater supplies many instances of the reinvigoration of the regular drama by the irregular forms. For example, the Italian comedy-of-masks seems to have originated in the humorous jesting of medieval village-festivals; and nothing could well be more frankly unliterary than these performances, since the plays were absolutely unwritten, the chief of the company explaining the plot to his companions, and the several comedians then improvising the dialog during the performance itself. Yet this comedy-of-masks was lifted into literature by Molière, whose first long play, the 'Étourdi,' is nothing more or less than a comedy-of-masks carefully written out in brilliant verse.

In like manner the melodrama, which had been elaborated year by year in the variety-shows of the eighteenth century fairs of Paris, served early in the nineteenth century as a model for the striking plays of Victor Hugo and of the elder Dumas. In Hugo's case the rather violent framework of the melodrama was so splendidly draped and decorated by his incomparable lyric magnificence that a critic so susceptible as Mr. Swinburne was moved to hail the French poet as of the race and lineage of Shakspere. The French melodrama and the Italian comedy-of-masks were each of them, at one stage of its career, almost as unliterary as the pantomimes of the Aleutians and the Australians; and yet we can see how each of them in turn has been elevated by a poet.

III

It is, perhaps, going a little too far to assert that the drama can be as independent of literature as painting may be, or as sculpture; and yet this is an overstatement only: it is not an untruth. The painter seeks primarily for pictorial effects, and the sculptor for plastic effects—just as the dramatist is seeking primarily for dramatic effects. On the other hand, there is no denying that the masterpieces of the graphic arts have all of them a poetic quality in addition to their pictorial and plastic qualities. To be recognized as master-pieces, they must needs possess something more than merely technical merits; but without these technical merits they would not be masterpieces. No fresco, no bas-relief, is fine because of its poetic quality alone. In like manner, we may be sure that there is no masterpiece of the drama in which the poetic quality, however remarkable it may be, is not sustained by a solid structure of dramaturgic technic. The great dramatist must be a poet, of course; but first of all he must be a theater-poet, to borrow the useful German term. And it is a German critic—Schlegel—who has drawn attention to the difference in dramatic capacity which subsists among nations equally distinguished for intellect, " so that theatrical talent would seem to be a peculiar quality, essentially distinct from the poetic gift in general." By the phrase " theatrical talent" Schlegel obviously means the dramaturgic faculty, the skill of the born play-maker. Voltaire says somewhere that the success of a poem lies largely in the choice of a subject; and it is even more certain that the success of a play lies in the choice of the special aspects of the subject which shall be shown in action on the stage. If the poet is not a play-wright, or if he cannot acquire the playwright's gift of picking out the scenes which will unfailingly move the hearts of the spectators, then his sheer poetic power will not save him, nor any affluence of imagery—just as no luxuriance of decoration would avail to keep a house standing if the foundations were faulty.

This dramaturgic faculty, without which the most melodious poet cannot hope to win acceptance as a dramatist, seems to be generally instinctive. It is a birthright of the play-maker, from whom it can sometimes be acquired by poets not so gifted by nature. For example, Victor Hugo was a poet who was not a born playwright, but who managed to attain the essential principles of the craft—essential principles which poets of the power and sweep of Byron and Browning were never able to grasp. These British bards were without the dramaturgic faculty which was possessed, in some measure, by the unliterary play-makers who devised the Italian comedy-of-masks.

In the early days of any art there is always imperfect differentiation; and the polychromatic bas-reliefs of the Egyptians remind us that it was long before painting and sculpture were separated. Not only are comedy and tragedy not carefully kept apart, but the drama itself is commingled with much that is not truly dramatic, and only by slow degrees is it able to disentangle itself from these extraneous matters. Even in the days of the great Greeks a lyric element sur-

17

vived in their tragedies which was often quite undramatic; and even in England, under Elizabeth, the stage was sometimes made to serve as a pulpit on which a sermon was preached, or as a platform on which a lecture was delivered, while the action of the play was forced to stand still.

There is also to be noted in every period of play-making a frequent element of mere spectacle. The rhythmic movements of the Greek chorus in the orchestra and their statuesque attitudes were meant to take the eye, like the coronation processions in the English chronicle-play of ' Henry VIII.' Anything of this sort is in its appropriate place in the masks of Ben Jonson and Inigo Jones, or in the *comédies-ballets* which Molière was so fertile in inventing for Louis XIV; but it is quite out of keeping with the serious drama, being wholly spectacular. Equally undramatic are the so-called " jigs " of the Elizabethan comic actors and the ground-and-lofty tumbling of the acrobatic performers who took part in the Italian comedy-of-masks. The persistent exhibition of trained animals of one kind or another, and their arbitrary inclusion within the story of the play itself, belongs to this frankly amusing aspect of theatrical entertainment. Here again the mere poet is likely to be unyielding where the born playwright is tolerant, sometimes even finding his account in this taste of the public for the tricks of an over-educated quadruped.　In the 'Two Gentlemen of Verona' Shakspere wrote a part for a trained dog, whereas it was a trained dog that led Goethe to resign the control of the Weimar theater; —but then, Goethe was a poet rather than a theater-poet.

IV

ALL these dogs and dances and processions are mere accidental accessories; and they have no vital relation to the fundamental principles of drama-turgy.　By slow degrees the dramatist gets control of his material, and comes to a conscious appreciation of the necessities of his art.　He may not be able to formulate the conditions which these necessities impose, but he has an intuitive perception of their requirements.　These drama-turgic principles are not mere rules laid down by theoretical critics, who have rarely any acquaintance with the actual theater; they are laws, inherent in the nature of the art itself, standing eternal, as immitigable to-day as when Sophocles was alive, or Shakspere, or Molière.　It is because these laws are unchanging that the observation of the modern theater helps to give us an insight into the methods of the ancient theater.　And we can go a step further, and confess that the latest burlesque in a music-hall, with its topical songs and its parodies, may be of immediate assistance to us in seizing the intent and in understanding the methods of Aristophanes.

To M. Ferdinand Brunetière—who profited, perhaps, by a hint of Hegel's—we owe the clearest statement of one important law only dimly perceived by earlier critics. He declares that the drama differs from the other forms of literature in that it must always deal with some exertion of the human will. If a play is really to interest us, it must present a struggle; its chief character must desire something, striving for it with all the forces of his being. Aristotle has defined tragedy as "the imitation of an action," but by action he does not mean mere movement—the fictitious bustle often found in melodrama and in farce. Perhaps the Greek critic intended *action* to be interpreted *struggle,* a struggle in which the hero knows what he wants, and wants it with all his might, and does his best to get it. He may be thwarted by some overpowering antagonist, or may be betrayed by some internal weakness of his own soul; but the strength of the play and its interest to the spectator will lie in the balance of the contending forces.

Prometheus, riveted to the rock, is determined, at any cost to himself, not to reveal the secret which the unjust god is seeking to wrest from him. Oedipus, the king, insists vehemently and irrevocably on discovering the secret that can bring only his own doom.   Romeo is headstrong to marry Juliet, and Juliet is bound to wed Romeo, no matter who says them nay, and in spite of the fierceness of the deadly feud of the two families.   Shylock purposes to have his pound of flesh, and he is not to be turned aside from his lust of revenge by any magnanimous appeals for mercy.   Tartuffe is resolved to go any length to get Orgon's money, and he is ready to run any risk to get Orgon's wife.   Lady Teazle is set on having her own way, and in gratifying her varying whims, even tho she ruins herself.

A determined will, resolute in seeking its own end, this is what we always find in the dramatic form; and this is what we do not find in the lyric or the epic.   In the lyric the poet is satisfied if he is able to set forth his own sentiment.   The epic poet—with whom the novelist must needs be classed nowadays—has to do mainly with adventure and with character.   His narrative is not necessarily dramatic; it may, if he should so prefer, be as placid as a mill-pond.   There is no obligation on the novelist to deal with what Stevenson has finely called the great passionate crises of existence "when duty and inclination come nobly to the grapple."   He may do so if he chooses, and if he does, his novel is then truly dramatic; but he need not deal with this conflict unless he likes, and not a few novels of distinction are not intended to be dramatic. Gil Blas, Tom Jones, and Waverley, Mr. Pickwick and Tartarin of Tarascon, Silas Lapham and Huckleberry Finn, are none of them beings of unfaltering determination, nor do they exert a controlling influence over the conduct of the stories to which they have given their names. Each of them is more or less a creature of accident and a victim of circumstance. No one of them is master of his own fate, or even steersman of his own bark on the voyage of life. M. Brunetière has drawn our attention to the many resemblances between 'Gil Blas' and the 'Marriage of Figaro' in local color and in moral tone; and then he points out that the comic hero of the novel is the sport of chance —he is passive; while the comic hero of the play is active, he has made up his mind to defend his bride against his master; and this struggle is the core of the comedy. The drama of Beaumarchais might be turned into a narrative easily enough; but the story of Lesage could never be made into a play. And here we may perceive a reason why the modern novel of character-analysis can very seldom be dramatized successfully.

This law of the drama formulated by M. Brunetière carries with it certain interesting corollaries. For example, if the drama demands a display of the human will, then we are justified in expecting to find the theater feeblest in the races of little energy and most flourishing among the more self-assertive peoples, and especially in the periods of their outflowering and expansion. This is precisely what we do find; and here we have the explanation of Schlegel's assertion that "in the drama nationality shows itself in the most marked manner." The native Egyptian has been the slave of many masters for scores of centuries, never strong enough of purpose to rise against them and rule himself; and to-day the fellahs of the valley of the Nile appear to be exactly what their ancestors were three and four thousand years ago. Since the dawn of history they seem never to have had souls of their own; and a careful search amid the abundant material in their museums fails to find any trace of a native drama.

The drama has no place in the existence of the weak-willed Egyptians; but it is likely to have a place of honor among the more determined nations, more particularly in the years that follow hard upon the most abundant expression of their vitality. And this is why we find the golden days of the drama in Greece just after Salamis; in Spain not long after the conquest of Mexico and Peru; in England about the time of the defeat of the Armada; and in France when Louis XIV was the foremost king of Europe. Golden days like these do not always follow the periods of energetic self-expression even among the most vigorous races, or else there would have been a noble dramatic literature in English in the nineteenth century, when both Great Britain and the United States were expanding exuberantly, but when the abundant vitality of the Americans and the British found other outlets than the theater. Yet it is only among the energetic races that the drama flourishes vigorously. If any people begins to relax its will and be languid, then its drama is likely soon to flag also and to become enfeebled; and this is what seems to have happened in France in the last quarter of the nineteenth century. If any people, virile enough in other ways, accepts a doctrine benumbing to the individual responsibility of man, it is not likely to develop a drama; and this is perhaps the reason why the theater did not establish itself among the sturdy Saracens, who bade fair more than once to overpower all Europe,—those valiant warriors having believed in foreordination rather than in free-will.

There is yet another corollary of this law of M. Brunetière's; or at least there is a chance to use it here to elucidate a principle often insisted upon by another French critic. The late Francisque Sarcey maintained that every subject for a play, every theme, every plot, contained certain possible scenes which the playwright was bound to present on the stage.   These he called the *scènes à faire*, the scenes which had to be done, which could not be shirked, but must be shown in action.   He asserted that the spectator vaguely desires these scenes, and is dumbly disappointed if they take place behind closed doors and if they are only narrated.   Now, if the drama deals with a struggle, then the incidents of the plot most likely to arouse and sustain the interest of the audience are those in which the contending forces are seen grappling with one another; and these are therefore the *scènes à faire*, the scenes that have to be set upon the stage before the eyes of the spectators.

Thus it is in the presence of the public that Sophocles brings Oedipus to the full discovery of the fatal secret he has persisted in seeking.   Thus Shakspere lets us behold a street-brawl of the Montagues and Capulets before making us witnesses of the love at first sight of Romeo and Juliet.   Nor is Shakspere satisfied to have some minor character tell us how Iago dropped the poison of jealousy into Othello's ear: he makes us see it with our own eyes,—just as Molière makes us hear Tartuffe's casuistical pleading with Orgon's wife.   One of the most obvious defects of French tragedy, especially in its decadence toward the end of the eighteenth century, is the frequent neglect or suppression of these necessary scenes and the constant use of mere messengers to narrate the episodes which the spectator would rather have beheld for himself. Victor Hugo remarked that at the performance of a tragedy of this type the audience was ever ready to say to the dramatist that what was being talked about seemed as tho it might be interesting—"then why not let us see it for ourselves?"

V

M. Brunetière's law helps us to perceive the necessary subject-matter of the drama; and M. Sarcey's suggestion calls our attention to the necessary presentation of the acutest moments of the struggle before our eyes. The drama has other laws also, due to the fact that it is an art; it has its conventions by which alone it is allowed to differ from nature. In every art there is an implied contract between the artist and the public, permitting him to vary from the facts of life, and authorizing him to translate these facts and to transpose them as his special art may require. The painter, so Mr. John La Farge has reminded us, arrests and stops upon a little piece of paper "the great depth and perspective of the world, its motion, its never resting"; while the sculptor transmutes "this soft, moving, fluctuating, colored flesh in an immovable, hard, rigid, fixed,

26

colorless material." As Goethe once tersely
phrased it, "Art is called art only because it is
not nature."

The conventions of the drama, its permitted
variations from the facts of life, are some of them
essential, and therefore eternal; and some of them
are accidental only, and therefore temporary. It
is a condition precedent to any enjoyment of a
play that the fourth wall of every room shall be
removed, so that we can see what is going on,
also that the actors shall keep their faces turned
toward us, and that they shall raise their voices so
that we can hear what they have to say. It is
essential, moreover, that the dramatist, having
chosen his theme, shall present it to us void of
all the accessories that would encumber it in real
life, showing us only the vital episodes, omitting
whatever may be less worthy of our attention,
and ordering his plot so that everything is clear
before our eyes, to enable us to understand at
once every fresh development as the story unfolds
itself. And as the action is thus compacted and
hightened, so must the dialog also be condensed
and strengthened. It is only a brief time that we
have to spend in the theater; and therefore must
the speech of every character be stripped of the
tautology, of the digressions, of the irrelevancies
which dilute every-day conversation.

These things are essential, and we find them

alike in the ancient drama and in the modern. But it is a matter of choice whether the characters shall employ prose or verse, Racine using rime, Calderon using assonance, and Shakspere using prose or verse or even rime as occasion serves. Verse and rime and assonance are all arbitrary variations from the customary speech of every day, but so also is the picked and polished prose of Sheridan, of Augier, and of Ibsen. Still further removed from the mere fact is the convention of the lyric drama—that all the characters shall sing, as tho song was their sole means of expression; and the convention of pantomime—that all the characters shall communicate with one another, and reveal their feelings to us, by gestures only, as tho the art of speech had not yet been elaborated.

Temporary and accidental conventions seem natural to us if we happen to be accustomed to them, but they strike us as grossly unnatural when they are unfamiliar. We do not object if a flimsy frame of canvas is lowered before our eyes to represent the castle of Elsinore, or if a stone wall suddenly becomes transparent that Faust may have a vision of Margaret. But we are inclined to smile at the black-robed attendant who hovers about the Japanese actor to provide a fan or a cushion, and who is supposed to be invisible or even non-existent. We should be taken aback if, after a murder was committed off the stage, a door suddenly flew open, revealing the criminals and the corpse posed in a living picture; and yet this is said to have been a device of the Greek theater. And we should laugh outright if we could listen to one of the medieval mysteries as they were acted in Portugal, when we heard the devil speaking Spanish, as it was always the custom of the Portuguese to represent him.

It is of these conventions that Sir Joshua Reynolds was thinking when he asserted that "in theatric representation great allowance must always be made for the place in which the exhibition is represented, for the surrounding company, the lighted candles, the scenes visibly shifted in our sight, and the language of blank verse so different from common English, which merely as English must appear surprising in the mouths of Hamlet and of all the court and natives of Denmark. These allowances are made; but their being made puts an end to all manner of deception." This last assertion we must qualify, since actual deception is no more the aim of the dramatic art than of the pictorial; in either case the illusion is ours only because we are willing that it should be. But when the painter requires us to make allowances for "the place in which the exhibition is represented," and also for "the surrounding company," he names two of the three conditions under which the playwright has to work perforce.

VI

As a drama is intended to be performed by actors, in a theater, and before an audience, the dramatist, as he composes, must always bear in mind the players, the playhouse, and the play-goers. The lyric poet needs to take thought only for the fit expression of his mood of the moment; and even the epic poet, if haply he had a patron, could be independent of his contemporaries. But no dramatic poet can be satisfied until he has seen his work in the theater itself, where his characters are made flesh and blood before his eyes, and where he can feel the thrill of the audience at his communicable emotion.

Of these three conditions in conscious conformity with which the dramatist labors, probably the least variable is the personality of the actor. The playhouse has taken many shapes in different climes, and the spectator must change with civilization itself; whereas the histrionic temperament is very much the same throughout the ages. It is well to remember that the actor must always do his work, not in private, like the poet or the painter, but in public, like the orator; and that the instrument of his art is always his own person. These are reasons why it is hard for him to escape self-consciousness. For the opportunity to perform he is dependent on the dramatist, altho he cannot help believing that he must understand the principles of his own art better than any one else. This is a reason why he may seem sometimes intolerant or overmasterful. But he loves his art loyally, and clutches eagerly at every chance to exercise it and to develop his own virtuosity. This loyalty of the actor the dramatists have always relied on; and his virtuosity they have always been glad to utilize. So it need surprise no one to be told that Sophocles was said to write his plays for a given actor, just as M. Sardou has composed certain of his pieces to fit a given actress. If we find that Hamlet is getting fat and scant of breath, we may wonder whether this was not, perhaps, because Burbage was putting on flesh about the time when Shakspere was revising the tragedy; and if we discover that a certain character in one of Molière's comedies has a limp, we may surmise that this is merely because the part was to be played by Béjart, the author's lame brother-in-law. It is this dependence of the dramaturgic artist on the histrionic which makes the drama so complex an art. The work of the dramatist can be revealed completely only by the labor of the actors; and one reason why there was no masterpiece of the drama in the middle ages is to be found in the fact that the medieval actors were all of them only amateurs.

However little the psychology of the tragic comedians has changed in the succeeding centuries, there have been many modifications in the shape and size and circumstances of the theaters in which they perform; and these modifications have exerted a potent influence on the successive forms of the drama. We can see one cause for the massive simplicity of Egyptian statuary in the fact that it had to be wrought in tough granite and in obstinate porphyry; and we can ascribe to the more delicate Parian marble a part, at least, of the exquisite perfection of Greek sculpture, while the capricious grotesquery of carving in the medieval cathedral may be due to the ease with which the friable sandstone of northern Europe could be worked. Perhaps the severe dignity of Greek tragedy was caused by the immense size of the Theater of Dionysus, where many thousand citizens gathered under the open sky; and, in like manner, may not some portion of the rapidity and variety of the Elizabethan drama have been due to the unadorned platform thrust out into the yard of the Globe Theater?

The tragedies of Shakspere were performed by daylight in a playhouse modeled on the courtyard of an inn and not wholly roofed; the com-

edies of Molière were brought out in an altered
tennis-court, on a shallow stage lighted by candles; the 'School for Scandal' was written for
the huge Drury Lane Theater, with its broad
proscenium-arch, dimly lit by flaring oil-lamps;
and the 'Gay Lord Quex' was produced in one
of the smaller theaters of London, with a proscenium like a picture-frame, brilliantly illumined
by the electric light.   After these examples it is
absurd to deny that the condition of the building
in which a play is performed may modify the
structure of the play itself.

Far more powerful than the influence of the
theater or of the actor upon the dramatist is
the influence of the audience, an influence not on
the form of the play, but on its substance.   As
those "who live to please must please to live," so
the play must be what the audience makes it.   If
the spectators are all coarse brutes, the drama
will be coarse and brutal; and if they are fun-
loving and free from sickly sentimentality, then
it is possible for the playwright to indulge in
romantic-comedy.   The drama is thus, of necessity, the most democratic of the arts; and any
attempt to organize it on an aristocratic basis—
such as Goethe ventured upon in Weimar—is
foredoomed to failure.   The drama appeals always to the broad public, and never to any self-
styled upper class.   A great poet may be haughty

and reserved, and ready to retire into an ivory tower; but a great dramatist must needs have an understanding of his fellow-man; he must have toleration and, above all, sympathy.

The influence of the spectator upon the play-wright is like the pressure of the atmosphere upon man: he may never even think about it, but all his organs are adjusted to it none the less. Schlegel remarked that "much must always depend on the capacities and humors of the audi-ence, and, consequently, on the national character in general, and the particular degree of mental culture"; and he might have gone further and asserted that the particular degree of moral culture was equally important. Before a Greek audience the husband of Alcestis could, without losing sympathy, accept his wife's offer to die in his stead—altho to us the fellow seems a pitiful coward. Before a Spanish audience the husband who is the 'Physician of his Own Honor' could, without losing sympathy, kill the wife whom he knows to be innocent, because there is a scandal about her—altho to us the man is merely a mur-derer. This sympathy of the audience is what even the most primitive playwright is always seeking. The Australian pantomime of the cattle-raid and the sham-fight would have failed to please if the natives had not at last beaten off the white men. In his 'Medea' Euripides apparently brought in Aegeus mainly that he might flourish a claptrap eulogy of Athens, the city where the play was to be acted; and in 'Henry V' Shakspere descends to a hyperbole of praise of England, which in the mouth of any one else might sound like the acme of jingoism.

The dramatist does not appeal to the spectators as individuals; he appeals to the audience as a whole, the audience having a collective soul which is not quite the same as the sum total of their several souls. A crowd, as such, is not a mere composite-photograph of its constituent persons; it has a certain personality of its own. By sheer force of juxtaposition the characteristics which the majority have in common are made more powerful, while the divergent characteristics of the individuals are subordinated or eliminated. When he is one of a multitude a man feels and thinks for the moment like the multitude, altho when he is alone again he may wonder why he yielded. As the dramatists must strive to arouse the emotions of the multitude, they cannot consider the special likings or the special knowledge of any single man or of any minor group of men. They must try to find the greatest common denominator of the throng. That is to say, they must ever seek the universal—for it is only at their peril that they can use the particular.

VII

DESIRING to please the audience as a whole, the dramatists are always ready to accept its verdict as final. There is no immediate appeal from this judgment, rendered in the theater itself, whether it is favorable or adverse. As Regnard makes the comedian say, "It is the public which determines the fate of works of wit—and our fate; and when we see it come in crowds to a new play we judge that the piece is good, and we do not care for any other assurance." And here the comedian was indisputably right; the approval of the public is the first proof of worthy success, for there are no good plays save those which have been applauded in the playhouse. The recognized masterpieces of the drama have all of them been popular in their own day. Sophocles and Shakspere, Lope de Vega and Molière, Sheridan and Beaumarchais, were, every one of them, widely appreciated by their contemporaries. True it is, also, that there have been other playwrights whose contemporary success was undeniable and whose fame is now faded—Heywood, for example, and Kotzebue and Scribe, in whose works posterity has failed to find the element of permanency.

Altho the works of Heywood and Kotzebue and Scribe call for no consideration from a lover of literature only, since purely literary merit is just what they lack, they still demand attention from a student of dramatic literature, who can spy out in them the selfsame qualities which gave immediate success also to the masterpieces of the great dramatists. The drama is an art which has developed slowly and steadily, and which is still alive; its history has the same essential unity, the same continuity, that we are now beginning to see more clearly in the history of the whole world. Its principles, like the principles of every other art, are eternal and unchanging, whatever strange aspects the art may assume. As history is said to be only past politics, and politics to be in fact only present history, so in dramatic litera-ture what once was helps us to understand what now is, and what now is aids us to appreciate what once was. If only we could behold all the links we should be able to trace an unbroken chain from the crudest mythological pantomime of primitive man down to the severest problem-play of the stern Scandinavian, whose example has been so stimulating to the modern stage.

II. GREEK TRAGEDY

I

THE distinguished French engineers who crossed the Atlantic in 1893 to study the wonders of the World's Fair in Chicago paused for a while in New York on their way, and were taken around the city to visit the most notable monuments of their art that the American metropolis had then to show. At the moment when the boat on which they were embarked, turning out of the North River, rounded the Battery and brought them at last in full view of the Brooklyn Bridge swung high in air beyond their heads, one of my scientific colleagues at Columbia University happened to be standing by the side of the foremost of the foreign visitors as they were captivated by the sudden vision of that splendid span thrown boldly across an arm of the sea. "How beautiful it is!" cried the Frenchman at once.—*Comme c'est beau !* Then, a moment later, he added, "How well done it is!"—*Comme c'est bien fait !* And finally, after he had looked long

38

and steadily, he said with redoubled admiration, "How well it is thought out!"—*Comme c'est bien étudié!*

Have we not here, in these sincere utterances, simply the three stages of admiration through which the expert must always pass in the stimulating presence of the consummate work of art? Its pure beauty will strike him at once; then he perceives the masterful skill of the craftsman who wrought it; and last of all he recognizes the solid labor underlying the skill and the beauty. And under no other circumstances do we pass so certainly through these stages of admiration as when we give ourselves to the contemplation of the masterpieces of the Greeks. It matters little what the art or what the scale of the work, unfailing felicity is what we find, and easy spontaneity, whether it is the tiny Temple of Nike or the Parthenon itself, whether it is a mere Tanagra figurine or the Winged Victory of Samothrace, whether it is a late idyl of Theocritus or a full-orbed tragedy of Sophocles.

Yet it would be very uncritical if we were to assume the Greeks to be so marvelously gifted by nature that they could grasp perfection at the first brave clutch for it. However incomparable the final achievements of the Greek people in sculpture, in architecture, and in the drama, the beginnings of these arts were as humble in Greece as anywhere else. Not a few temples must have been put together more or less clumsily, before the Parthenon could raise its superb beauty on the steep Acropolis; and many a hundred of the ruder archaic statues served to train the eye and the hand of the sculptors before they could compass the power and the grace of the Hermes. The masterpieces survive for our constant delight; while the primitive attempts that failed to satisfy even the crude taste of those who wrought them —these have vanished or are neglected. We are now coming to see, however, that these earlier efforts are invaluable aids for the fuller appreciation of the final masterpieces. As Haeckel has reminded us, the mind of an educated man of the highest civilized races is "the last link of a long ancestral chain, and the innumerable older and inferior links are indispensable for its proper understanding." Adequately to esteem the true value of Sophoclean tragedy, we need to know the obscure root from which it sprang, and to trace its growth from the prehistoric past.

II

A RECENT investigator into the beginnings of the arts, Professor Hirn, holds the drama to be the earliest of them all; and he goes so far as to suggest that a rude pantomime, accompanied perhaps by a dance, or by a rhythmic chant, may be older even than language itself. Very early among the Greeks we get hints of a miracle-play in honor of Demeter; and perhaps in this we may see a germ of the later drama, since whatever may have preceded it is now hopelessly beyond our knowledge, altho we may hazard a guess that it had been evolved slowly out of a panto-mimic dance, probably at first without spoken words. It was in the springtime that the festi-val of Demeter was celebrated; and in the fall, when the grapes were trodden out, the vine-clad Dionysus had his turn with revelry and joyous song and orgiastic dance. It is from religious exercises, set off always with music and often with dancing, that the drama has evolved itself in almost every literature—in Chinese, for ex-ample, and again in Sanskrit. The development of a true drama does not always take place—ap-parently not in Hebrew literature, for one; but if it does, then this is its source always. "By the simultaneous employment of mimicry, song, speech, and instrumental music," so Professor Letourneau declares, "the opera-ballet of the early ages was the form of esthetics most fitted strongly to impress spectators and actors, and at the same time to satisfy a very lively psychical want, that of projecting mental images outward, of reproducing, with all the relief of reality, what exists in the brain only in the state of recollection or desire. The civilized theater is only the natural development of this opera-ballet; and it preserves an equal attraction and an equal power even after losing the lyrical form which dated from its origin."

In the civilized theater of the Greeks the drama never wholly gave up the lyrical form it inherited from the remote ancestor which M. Letourneau terms the opera-ballet of savage tribes. It grew out of one or another of the Dionysiac commemorations; of this we may be certain, altho we must be doubtful as to the successive stages of its expansion. The information we get from Aristotle is painfully summary. "Tragedy," he tells us, "as also comedy, was at first mere improvisation. The one originated with the leaders of the dithyramb, the other with those of the phallic songs. . . . Tragedy advanced by slow degrees: each new element was in turn developed." The dithyramb was a swinging hymn to Dionysus sung by a chorus of youths sometimes somewhat under the influence of the new wine. At first this chorus was but a band of revelers, with an impromptu chant fitted rudely to the dance they were devising spontaneously. The most striking of these impromptu chants would tend to become traditional, thereafter to be varied from only on hints from the more inventive of the young fellows—much as to-day, in a negro camp-meeting, we may hear new words fitted to an air which itself is in process of modification.

In time the most ingenious member of the chorus would be recognized as the leader, and he would be expected to "line out" the songs and to conduct the dance to the music of the flute. We are told that it was Arion who earliest of all wrote out the lyrics which had hitherto been more or less improvised, and, to balance them, strophe and antistrophe. Arion also it may have been who first put the singers into the costume of satyrs, making them a band of followers accompanying Dionysus himself. Their faces were stained with the wine-lees, in honor of the god perhaps, and yet it may be that this was to give a fuller freedom to the individual, emboldened by this elementary disguise—just as an American boy is far less shamefaced when he uses burnt cork to black up as a negro-minstrel than when he takes part in any ordinary private theatricals.

The differentiation of the leader from the chorus would allow a colloquy between the leader and the chorus; and the leader might in time be moved to act out a part of the legend of the god's life while the chorus commented lyrically or else took part in the action. But the most important step remained to be taken; and this is ascribed to Thespis. The poet who was already the leader became also an actor, not always personating a single character, but assuming several characters in turn. To enable him to disguise himself he wore a different mask for each of the several characters he undertook, this device being suggested to him perhaps by the fact that the priest of Demeter always wore a mask at her mysteries. From the moment when the play was thus peopled by several characters, even tho they were presented one after the other and never two together, a plot was possible, however slight: a complete action could be shown, however elementary; and the struggle essential to the true dramatic form could be represented before the spectators to arouse their sympathy.

The poet-leader of the chorus having been developed into an actor, the chorus promptly raised another of their members to take his place as their chief, just as we see in the history of modern music how the conductor differentiated himself slowly from the other instrumentalists, and how, when he stood wholly apart from them, one of the first violins was designated in his stead as concertmaster. The lyrics of the chorus existed thereafter not only for their own sake, but also that they might fill out the time while the actor was making his exchange of one character for another.

This increasing complexity came a little before or a little after another step in advance; the play itself was no longer improvised on the spur of the moment; it was composed carefully, and written out and committed to memory both by the actor and by the chorus. The purely popular entertainment extemporized annually at a vintage-festival began to be a work of art; and literature came to the aid of the theater. And at about the same time this elementary drama, destined to so splendid a development, gave up its nomadic career and established itself in Athens.

"The country is lyric," so Longfellow declared, "and the town dramatic." The lyrist may relieve his own feelings in song with no need for a listener; but the dramatist must conceive his utterances always with a consciousness of their effect when repeated before a crowd. It may be that Thespis, who was an Icarian, headed a company of strollers performing at village-festivals, and fixing itself finally in Athens at the invitation of Pisistratus, the enlightened despot then striving to make his city the home of all the arts. At first Thespis gave his performances as a private enterprise, much as Molière did when he brought back to Paris the company he had trained during his long years of wandering in the provinces. But the Greeks liked everything to be done decently and in order, and they joyed always in a competition of any kind. These are probably the reasons why the state took over the control of the drama. Thereafter tragedy was performed at the City Dionysia, the great spring-festival of the Athenians, when the visitors thronged there from all parts of Greece. In the course of time different dramatists were invited to present, each on separate days, groups of tragedies; and the cost of producing each group was borne by a rich citizen, who paid for the training of the chorus, for the costumes, for the musicians, and for all the accessories of adequate stage-management. There was in Athens then a high sense of civic duty, as, indeed, there seems to be now, when the stranger marvels to note how many public buildings have of late been given to the city by one or another of her loyal sons.

The early dithyrambic chorus performed its evolutions around an altar to Dionysus, in the market-place, probably; and when the leader began to hold colloquies with his fellows, a platform was put up for him in the center of the circle and at the side of the altar. When the leader became an actor, playing various parts one after the other, a booth of skins was erected behind the platform, so that he could change his mask and his costume out of sight of the spectators. But as this booth would surely hide him from the view of some of those standing all around, the circle of spectators was broken at one point, to which the booth and the platform were moved back. In front of this new focus of attention at least two thirds of the circular space remained free for the movements of the chorus. Beyond this open area, which was known as the orchestra, the seats for the spectators were fanned out on three sides. The low platform whereon the actor appeared in front of the booth was the only stage, and there was no scenery.

The circling seats for the audience were but temporary erections, perhaps not unlike the tiers of benches seen in our traveling circuses; and they were not always stable. Probably this is one reason why the market-place was abandoned for a hollow of the hill that towered high over the city. At the bottom a circular space was leveled to serve as an orchestra, and above it, in concentric rows up the sides of the curving slope, seats of wood or of stone were arranged. As the spectators were now so placed that every one had a full view of the whole orchestra, there was no longer any need for the platform on which the actor had stood. The booth of skins was replaced by a more commodious wooden hut, in which the costumes of the actor would be better protected from the weather, and the roof of which could be utilized later in the development of the drama by a god looking down on men below, or by a watchman on the housetop—very much as the gallery over the stage was made serviceable by the Elizabethan playwrights.

III

VERY conjectural indeed must be any attempt to set forth the successive steps by which a song-and-dance of village revelers grew into a lofty tragedy of a stateliness worthy of the noble city where it was at last established. Arion is no more than a myth, and Thespis is at best only a tradition; but Aeschylus is a fact at last. It was Aeschylus who, so Aristotle informs us, "first introduced a second actor; he diminished the importance of the chorus, and assigned the leading part to the dialog." As the first actor could personate several characters, so also could the second; and thereafter the dramatist was at liberty to people his play as amply as he chose, subject to the sole limitation that only two of the personages of the drama should appear at the same time. Aeschylus could well afford to diminish the importance of the chorus, since he had now the power to put before the spectators the two opposing characters in whom was embodied the struggle which was the backbone of the plot.

When the actually dramatic was thus made possible the poet had less need of the merely lyric. With the aid of the two actors he could present in action the culminating episodes of the essential struggle, the *scènes à faire* (to use Sarcey's invaluable term), the scenes that must be shown if the story is to hold the interest of the audience.

The Greek dramatic poets never wholly relinquished the lyric, out of which the dramatic was evolving itself; but the former became less and less important as the latter came slowly to an understanding of its own powers and possibilities. When we arrange the extant tragedies in chronological order we cannot fail to discover several stages of artistic growth, from the semi-lyric 'Suppliants' of Aeschylus to the perfectly proportioned and vitally dramatic 'Oedipus' of Sophocles, with a later decline almost into melodrama in the 'Medea' of Euripides. Semi-lyric the 'Suppliants' is, and only semi-dramatic; it seems to represent Greek tragedy as it was before Aeschylus had discovered how to bring out the dramatic elements inherent in his theme. To the chorus was given more than half of the words spoken; and if only a few slight modifications were made, a single actor could take all the characters in turn. It was possibly the very first play ever performed on the site of the stately Theater of Dionysus, to be erected more than a century

49

the maidens sing an ode of lamentation. Now enters the Herald of the suitors (the first actor, who had previously impersonated Danaus), and he sternly bids the young women follow him to the ship, giving no heed to their terrified appeals for mercy. The King of Argos returns, and a bitter battle of words follows between him and the Herald, after which both of them withdraw, whereupon the chorus expresses, in a song, its joy that the monarch has refused to surrender them. At last Danaus comes back (the first actor once more) to conduct his daughters into the city itself for greater security. The maidens follow their father out of the orchestra, and the play is over.

If the dispute between the King of Argos and the Herald had been narrated by a witness, and not actually presented, then only one actor would be required for the performance of the 'Suppliants,' one actor personating in turn each of the characters. But without this dispute the play would be less dramatic than it is; and even now its lyric abundance is what we notice first, the adroit alternation of hymn and song and ode. Yet there is a struggle sustaining these interludes and justifying their existence; there is that conflict of will which is the very essence of the drama. The daughters of Danaus are determined not to marry their cousins—who are resolved that they shall; and here the issue is joined, and we have the possibility of dramatic interest. There is even suspense, since the spectators are in doubt, first, whether the King of Argos will promise the protection sought, and second, whether he will afterward yield to the arrogant demands of the pursuers.

In the later plays of Aeschylus, devised for performance under similar conditions of theatrical simplicity,—an open orchestra with no stage and no scenery, with two actors only, with a full chorus of fifteen men,—in these we see the same imperfect differentiation of what is dramatic from what is lyric. In one of them, the 'Persians,' we cannot really discover, in the episodes of the play as we have it, any element of a conflict of will. In another, 'Prometheus Bound,' we can see at the core of it the strife between Zeus (who wishes to wrest a fatal secret from the mortal) and Prometheus (who will stubbornly endure all the tortures he knows to be in store for him sooner than disclose what he has resolved to keep hid). In a third tragedy, 'Agamemnon,' also to be performed by two actors only, one of them impersonating Clytemnestra, and the other appearing in turn as the Watchman, as the Herald, as Agamemnon, as Cassandra, and as Aegisthus —in this tragedy the struggle is more dramatically presented, with a more skilful use of suspense.

Indeed, so artfully has Aeschylus ordered the sequence of his plot that almost from the beginning the spectator is oppressed by an awful sense of impending doom. With all its meagerness of incident, the play is never lacking in theatrical effectiveness; it is not only truly tragic, it is also really dramatic.

IV

AFTER Thespis, about whom we know almost nothing, other play-makers had come—Pratinas and Phrynichus, about whom we know something. As they had prepared the path for Aeschylus, so Aeschylus made the way ready for Sophocles, in whom the Greek theater had its most accomplished artist. Aristotle tells us that it was Sophocles who first made use of a third actor, thus setting an example followed by all who came after him, and who did not dare ask for more actors than Sophocles had been satisfied with. In Aeschylus we see the drama emerging out of the lyric and seeking hesitatingly to differentiate itself. In Sophocles we see the drama solidly established, and yet supported and relieved by lyric interludes which are made integral parts of a harmonious structure. He was no violent reformer, and, indeed, it may be that he was almost unconscious of the importance of his improvements. Certain of his tragedies are as undramatic as certain of the tragedies of Aeschylus. But in 'Oedipus the King,' on the other hand, he showed how a Greek tragedy can retain much of its primitive simplicity of outline and yet express a gradually increasing intensity of emotion, until at last the action rises to its inevitable and appalling catastrophe.

With a third actor in addition to the two used by Aeschylus, Sophocles could present two characters arguing face to face, with a third intervening to change the current of the discussion. He could reduce to a minimum all mere narration by messengers; and he could show before the eyes of the spectators the *scènes à faire*, the salient episodes of the vital struggle which was the heart of his theme, as when Antigone stands up against Creon, asserting that she did only her duty when she bestowed funeral rites upon her dead brother, whatever the consequences to herself for thus violating the King's decree. Sophocles made use of the chorus not only as a device to gain time while the actors were changing from one character to another,·and not merely to relieve the stress of the action by quieter passages of pure lyric when no actors were present;· but in his hands the members of the chorus were made subordinate personages of the play, closer to the chief characters than the spectator was, and therefore serving as intermediaries for the com-

number of actors to three and added scene-painting; but no two authorities are in agreement as to what we are to understand by the last word thus translated. Scene-painting as we know it nowadays, this is something which it is quite impossible for Sophocles to have anticipated. Aristotle's phrase may mean no more than that the dressing-house owed to the suggestion of Sophocles a more seemly appearance, and perhaps even some symbolic decoration, in accord with the time and place of the successive tragedies which were to be performed before it. Very likely the various plays of Sophocles were originally acted in an orchestra (which was a circular space about seventy feet in diameter), and before a dressing-house about as long as the orchestra was wide, and provided with three doors opening on the same level. Altho Attic audiences were like Elizabethan audiences in that their prime interest was in what was to be acted before them, and in that they never gave a needless thought to the special spot where the action was supposed to take place, still the presence of a low-lying edifice beyond the orchestra might be useful, not only by confining the roving eye of the spectator, but as suggesting to him the palace or the temple in front of which the story was to be acted.

'Oedipus the King,' which is the masterpiece of Sophocles, and indeed of all Attic tragedy,

begins with the slow and solemn entrance of the
chorus of Theban elders into the orchestra.   Then
the center doors of the dressing-house open and
Oedipus comes forth (the first actor).   He seems
taller than an ordinary man, because he has on the
buskin (or tragic boot), and because he is wearing
the lofty tragic mask, which rises high above his
own head.   He asks what it is they want of
him, and he is answered by a Priest of Zeus (the
second actor), who beseeches the King to find
some remedy for the plague that besets the
people.   Oedipus replies that he has already sent
his brother-in-law, Creon, to consult the oracle.
Then enters Creon (the third actor) with good
news: the blight will cease when vengeance is
done on the murderer of Laïus (who was the
predecessor of Oedipus, and whose widow,
Iocasta, Oedipus has taken to wife).   Creon and
the Priest of Zeus withdraw, but Oedipus remains while the chorus intones a prayer; and
then he promises a reward for the name of the
murderer of Laïus, and declares that he has sent
for Tiresias, the blind prophet.   Tiresias enters
(the third actor again, but now wearing a different mask); he seeks to avoid making any disclosure, until Oedipus loses patience and accuses
him of being a partner in the crime, whereupon
the seer declares that Oedipus himself is the
guilty one.

Certain of his own innocence, Oedipus suspects Creon of having suborned Tiresias to make this charge. But the blind prophet asserts his own independence, and warns Oedipus that "this day shall show thy birth and shall bring thy ruin." Tiresias departs, Oedipus withdraws into the house, and the chorus sings a hymn of foreboding. Then returns Creon (the third actor), and Oedipus comes out to upbraid him with treachery. They are now joined by Iocasta (the second actor, who has, of course, changed his mask also), and at his wife's appeal Oedipus modifies his sentence of death against her brother to one of banishment. When Creon has departed, Iocasta asks the cause of the quarrel; and then reveals to Oedipus that her first husband, Laïus, was warned that he should die by the hand of his own son, and that the father therefore caused the child to be thrown from a cliff. Oedipus inquires how it was that Laïus died, and then he begins to perceive it to be dimly possible that he himself may be the slayer of his wife's first husband. Oedipus tells Iocasta that he was brought up by the King of Corinth, but was once taunted with the fact that he was not a true son, whereupon he had gone to the oracle, which had warned him that he should marry his own mother, in fear of which sin he had abandoned Corinth. The King and Queen withdraw together in doubt and sorrow, and the chorus chants a song of destiny.

Iocasta comes forth on her way to prayer, when there arrives a Messenger from Corinth (the third actor once more), who announces the death of the King of Corinth. Iocasta has Oedipus summoned, and together they question the Messenger, who, to relieve their minds, discloses that Oedipus was only the adopted son of the dead monarch, and that he himself had received Oedipus as a babe from a servant of Laïus. Iocasta, after vainly imploring her husband to seek no further, herself perceives the fatal truth—that she is married to her own son after he had killed his father. With a sudden cry of despair she rushes within and is seen no more. Oedipus, still groping, confronts the Messenger from Corinth with an old Herdsman of Laïus (the second actor again), and forces the aged servitor to admit that instead of destroying the child of Iocasta and Laïus, as he was bidden, he had spared the boy and given it to the man who is now present as the Messenger from Corinth. At last Oedipus sees that the oracles are fulfilled, and that he is truly accursed. Overwhelmed with woe, he totters into the house, whereupon the chorus sings an ode on the uncertainty of life.

Then comes one from within (the second actor), to relate the suicide of Iocasta, who has hanged herself, and to announce also the punishment which Oedipus has inflicted on himself for his unwitting sins: he has thrust out both his eyes. Oedipus soon enters, probably wearing a different mask, and he bewails his miserable fate, while the chorus sympathizes. Next Creon returns to assume the throne, but not to reproach his stricken brother-in-law. Oedipus is about to go forth a wanderer on the face of the earth, and Creon allows him to bid farewell to his two little daughters, confided thereafter to the care of their uncle. And when Oedipus and his children have withdrawn with Creon, the chorus gravely sums up the moral and warns the spectators that they are to "call no man happy until he is dead." Then they themselves circle slowly out of the orchestra to the sad and piercing music of the flute, and disappear at length behind the dressing-house; and the play is done at last.

When Aristotle declared that tragedy is a higher art than the epic, it was of this masterpiece of Sophocles that he was thinking. Altho there are here, in a single plot, parricide and incest and suicide, horrible crimes linked in an inexorable chain, so austere is the treatment and so lofty the purpose that the play is void of offense. It is full of terror, and it is charged with pity, for not from fate alone does Oedipus suffer. His punishment is also for his own pride and wilful-

ness; and his downfall is brought about because
he insisted on discovering what it was best for
him never to know.   To exert one's own will is
the final proof of man's existence; and therefore
what the drama necessarily deals with is the most
significant action of human life.   This essential
struggle Sophocles brings out more sharply than
Aeschylus before him or than Euripides after him.

That a tragedy such as 'Oedipus the King'
could delight and move the thousands of spectators who sat in the seats that girt the orchestra,
or who stood higher up on the hillside—this is
testimony to the artistic sensibility of the Athenian
audience and to its trained intelligence.   The dramatist must always conform to the taste of those
to whom he is appealing.   He may seek to improve that taste, to elevate it and purify it, but
he cannot ignore it.   If he fails to consider it, his
play will fail also.   He is fortunate if his audience
is made up of all sorts and conditions of men, not
the educated only, or the ignorant either, but
broadly chosen; for the more various the spectators, the more bravely can the dramatist deal with
the universal element of life.

Professor Jebb has reminded us that "the collective impression of intelligent listeners . . . has
a critical value of a kind which can seldom be
claimed for the judgment of any single critic";
and he adds that "in the case of a people with the

unique gifts of the Greek race,—their obedience to reason, and their instinct for beauty,—the critical value of the collective impression was exceptionally high." The Greek dramatist felt this solidarity with the whole body of spectators whom he was to delight and to thrill; he was certain of a sympathetic understanding of his boldest effort; and by this certainty he could not fail to be stimulated.

The beauty which Sophocles sought to set before the Athenian audience was not only a union of the lyric and the dramatic, sustained by music: it was pictorial also and plastic. The taste of the spectators was as keenly critical of the sculpturesque attitudes of the actors or of the chorus as it was trained to appreciate the delivery of a phrase, the rhythm of a line, the propriety of a speech, or the structure of the plot. The dramatist was responsible for the whole performance, for the complete art-work. It was his duty and his delight himself to drill the chorus in their maneuvers, and to see that the gestures were ever graceful and the groupings always harmonious.

Among us who speak English the opera is the privilege of the rich, with all the narrowing and limitation that therefore ensues; but if it was not thus restricted in its scope, one might dwell at length on a certain likeness between the tragedies of Sophocles and the music-dramas of Wagner,

from which, indeed, they are less remote in form
and in spirit than they are from the plays of
Shakspere as these are now performed.   Wagner
was following Sophocles in seeking a simplicity
of theme as massive as it is splendid, and also in
wishing to add to the lyric and the dramatic all
the further beauty to be derived from a skilful
use of the plastic art.   Wagner could avail himself of scenery and of artificial lighting and of
various mechanical devices impossible to Sophocles; but undoubtedly the Greek dramatist, like
the German composer, relied upon the contemplation of characteristic attitudes and upon the
appropriate positions of the actors and of the
chorus.   The ancient dramatist had even one
advantage over the modern in that his plays were
performed out of doors in the springtime, when
at any moment a breeze might sweep up from
the sea to flutter the flowing draperies of the
characters and of the chorus, and to blow their
loose garments about their bodies in lines of
unexpected beauty.

V

ON the serene heights of dramatic poesy, where
Sophocles breathed freely as tho there only could
he find his native air, the third of the great Greek
dramatists was ill at ease; and in the plays of
Euripides we can perceive at least the beginning

63

of a decline. The structure of his plots is less careful; the situations are more violent; the characters are less worthy of pity; the moral tone of the whole work is less elevated and far less inspiriting. If we admit that Aeschylus dealt with demigods, and that Sophocles honored heroes, while Euripides is interested rather in men as they are, we must acknowledge also that man as Euripides represents him is often a pitiful creature, involved in sensational adventures far less significant than those to be found in the earlier tragedies. Indeed, it is woman rather than man whom Euripides likes to take as the chief figure of his pathetic story—a woman often of unbridled passions and swift to act on the primary impulses of her sex.

Despite all the evidence of the extreme cleverness of Euripides, we can see that he was not a born play-maker like Sophocles; he had not the same instinctive certainty of touch; and he seems also to have neglected the art of composition. Even when by chance he has made choice of a story in which there is a set struggle, such as would give substance to a plot, he sometimes fails to present the *scènes à faire*, the scenes which must be shown in action if the spectator is to find full satisfaction. His plays are frequently melodramatic in their framework, while the poet is ironic in his treatment of his theme, a combination which could not but be disconcerting to the Athenian public. His tragedies are lacking in the noble sincerity to be found in the tragedies of Sophocles, and they are also not so homogeneous, being sometimes without the unity of design and even without the unity of tone to which the Greeks had been accustomed. The Attic distaste for the abnormal and for the freakish will help to explain the failure of Euripides to please his immediate contemporaries; and it is evidence of a later decline of the Greek delicacy of perception that a wide popularity did come to Euripides shortly after his death.

To-day our taste is not Attic, and even by taking thought we cannot put ourselves in the place of the Athenian, to see his poets as he saw them, and to weigh them in the equal scales. And this is why many lovers of literature find Euripides the most modern of the great Greeks, the least remote in his attitude toward our common humanity, the closest to us in emotion and in character-drawing. His plays may be less tragic than those of his greater predecessors, less severe, even less artistic. But we are not so particular as the Athenians were; our standards of taste are not so lofty; and we relish a broader pathos than appealed to the Greeks. Even if certain of the plays of Euripides are not tragedies truly, but tragi-comedies or melodramas or domestic dramas, they are only the more modern for that. Nowadays we are glad to greet a heroine who has sinned and suffered, and whose sad situation is so presented as to wring our hearts with sympathy and to keep us dissolved in tears. Medea, for example, is perhaps the earliest " woman with a past "; she is the ancestress of the ' Dame aux Camélias ' and of ' Magda '; and the tragedy of Euripides is like the dramas of Dumas and Sudermann in that it is little more than a star-part, a piece intended for the exploitation of a single actor, — as a brief summary will make plain.

The Nurse of Medea's children (the second actor) enters the orchestra from the house, and opens the play with a long speech, telling the spectators how hard it is for Medea to bear the new marriage which her husband Iason is about to make. The Teacher of Medea's children (the third actor) leads on the two boys, and informs the Nurse that Medea and her children are to be sent away. Before the Teacher takes the boys into the house Medea is heard bemoaning her fate. A chorus of Corinthian women now enters the orchestra and asks the Nurse why Medea is crying aloud. At the summons of the Nurse, Medea (the first actor) comes forth and exposes the reasons for her grief. Then enters Creon (the third actor again), King of Corinth, and father of the maiden Iason is about to wed. He informs

66

Medea that she is banished with her children. She begs a day's delay before her departure; and Creon at last grants this just before he goes. The chorus chants the degeneracy of the times.

Iason (the second actor) enters, soon revealing himself to be a contemptible creature. He is scolded and threatened by Medea. Even the chorus comments adversely on his feeble self-defense; and when he withdraws the chorus sings a hymn to love. Aegeus (the third actor) arrives; he is an Athenian, and with him Medea agrees to fly on his promise of shelter and protection. When he is gone Medea declares her intention of killing the bride of Iason, and the chorus mildly dissuades her. She retires to get a poisoned robe; and the chorus sings a stirring ode to the glory of Athens. Medea comes back, and so does Iason (the second actor as before), whom she has sent for. She calls her children to bear the robe to Creon's daughter, that she may entreat Creon to allow the boys to remain. After the chorus has sung another song of condolence with Medea, the Teacher brings back the two boys, and the mother weeps over them, and bids them farewell.

Suddenly a Messenger (the third actor) rushes in to bid Medea fly, since the poison has destroyed both Creon and his daughter. Medea rejoices, and, for further revenge on her false husband, she is now resolved to slay her two boys also. She goes within the house, and we hear the outcry of the children, while the chorus expresses its disapproval of her deadly act. Iason comes back, and the chorus informs him of what evil deed Medea has just been guilty. He orders the doors to be broken in, whereupon Medea appears on the roof of the dressing-house, and is borne away through the air in a chariot drawn by dragons—probably represented by a basket of some sort swung high in the air by a rope from a crane at the end of the dressing-house. After Medea has disappeared Iason exhales his woe and departs, followed by the chorus, declaring that the gods do things for reasons inscrutable to mortals.

As we contemplate the evolution of Greek tragedy, we see that the austere Aeschylus, inheriting a form semi-lyric and only semi-dramatic, felt his chorus to be at least as important as were his actors; we see that the sincere Sophocles, developing the dramatic element, was yet able to make the chorus helpful, in that it served to suggest to the spectators the feelings he wished them to have; and we see that the skeptic Euripides found the chorus a useless survival which he did not dare discard out of respect for tradition, and of which he availed himself mainly for the display of his own lyric gift. He might be a careless playwright, a brutal realist, a frank sensationalist; he was an exquisite lyrist. As Coleridge said, his choruses "may be faulty as choruses, but how beautiful and affecting they are as odes and songs!"

VI

THE presence of the chorus in the orchestra throughout the play accounts for the fact that the Greek dramatists scarcely ever attempted any change of scene in the course of a tragedy. For one thing, there was no scenery to change; and for another, there was no easy way of making plausible a substitution of one imagined place for another while the chorus remained stationary before the eyes of the spectators; so here we have a valid reason for what is called the Unity of Place. And the absence of any intermission during the performance of a tragedy—due also, in part at least, to the presence of the chorus—led to a straightforward movement of the plot, one episode following close on another, the intervening choral odes allowing for whatever lapse of time might be required by the plot. These extensions of the duration of the action being taken for granted, and not actually specified, many critics have seen in Greek tragedy what is called the Unity of Time.

The circumstances of the actual performance will also account for most of the other peculiarities of the Greek plays; and if, for instance, we find in them few scenes of violence, of physical excitement, of battle, murder, and sudden death, probably one reason is that combats and rapid motion of any kind were difficult to actors raised on the buskin and partly blinded by the towering tragic mask. To fall to the ground in these accoutrements would be to risk the ungraceful and to break up the stately harmony and sculptural beauty of gesture and of grouping, like that of a bas-relief, which was called for by the mingling of the actors and of the chorus in front of the low-lying dressing-house as a background.

The same circumstances of the actual performance which made the Greek dramatist seem to be bound by the so-called Unities of Time and Place forced him to deal only with the culminating moments of his plot, so compacted in the presentation that more than one ancient tragedy appears to be little longer than the fifth and final act of a modern play. As all that went before had to be explained briefly in the earlier scenes, the Greek was debarred from exhibiting the development or the disintegration of a character such as can occur only after a lapse of time. All his characters are and must be unchanging. Prometheus and Medea are the same at the end of the play as they were at the beginning, and they retain always the same fixed mask. Even Oedipus, who alters his mask, and is broken and bowed with shame and grief in the sight of the spectators, has had no time yet to realize the full force of his dread discovery. Yet the disadvantage of this was lessened by the fact that every Greek dramatist presented on the same day four plays, the last being satiric, and the first three being sometimes so linked together as to show successive incidents of the same legend. The four plays followed one after the other, filling the long spring day with pleasure; and in the intervals, no doubt, the vast multitude on the hillside around the sunken ring of the orchestra rose to their feet and stretched their limbs and refreshed themselves with meat and drink,—in much the same fashion as the latter-day pilgrims to Bayreuth are now wont to do.

It is in the chorus that we must see not only the germ, but the dominating influence of Greek tragedy. The chorus survived to the end as the ever-present evidence that tragedy had been developed out of the dithyramb. The early spectators who gathered in the market-place to listen to the Dionysiac lyrics were delighted with even a mere hint of the drama; and in the beginning no one had yet acquired the skill needed to hold the interest of an audience by the artful cumulation of dramatic episodes. In the beginning the 'Suppliants,' which has little more action than an oratorio, and the 'Persians,' which appears quite undramatic to us, because we are looking back, may have seemed dramatic to the Greeks, because they were looking forward—because these plays, chiefly lyric as they are, are also nearer to the true drama than anything that had gone before. The undramatically distended lamentations of 'Philoctetes,' even, were probably more interesting than a choral ode would have been, if only because they came as a relief between two choral odes. Aristotle traces the slow improvement with his customary clearness: "It was not till late that the short plot was discarded for one of greater compass. . . . The number of episodes was also increased, and other embellishments added."

The simplicity and the dignity which we admire in Greek tragedy are due partly to the circumstances of its origin. They are due partly, also, to the Greek's gifts, to his inventiveness, to his ingenuity, to his sense of form, to his desire for order and harmony and symmetry. Crude in certain ways the Greek drama is, as we cannot help admitting; but still it is the most wonderful in all the long history of the theater, because it is the only great drama which has been wrought out by a single people, wholly without any aid from the outside, with absolutely no model to profit by. The dramatic instinct, the desire to personate, the enjoyment of mimicry—these things are inherent in all of us: savages and children possess them abundantly; and yet the Greeks were alone in their artistic utilization of these natural qualities, and in so availing themselves of these that they were able to develop a drama, and to raise this drama to the loftiest reaches of poetry, entirely on their own initiative. This they did, and this no modern race has been able to do, because the dramatic literature of every modern language has come, at one time or another, directly or indirectly, under the influence of Greek tragedy.

III. GREEK AND ROMAN COMEDY

I

THE law of the theater, as M. Brunetière has formulated it, is that the drama must deal with an exercise of the human will, and that therefore a struggle of some sort is an essential element in the pleasure we take in a play. A clear understanding of this law is helpful in any question of classification—for example, in the difficult attempt sharply to set off tragedy from melodrama and comedy from farce. If the obstacle against which the will of the hero finally breaks itself is absolutely insurmountable, the Greek idea of fate, for example, the Christian decree of Providence, or the modern scientific doctrine of heredity, then we have tragedy pure and simple. If the obstacle is not absolutely insurmountable, being no more than the social law, something of man's own making and therefore not finally inexorable, then we have the serious drama. If the obstacle is only the desire of another human being, then the result of the contention of these two characters is likely to give us a comedy. And if the obstacle is merely one of the minor conventions of society, then we may have farce. But as there is no hard-and-fast line separating these several obstacles which the several heroes are struggling to overcome, so the different types of play may shade into one another, until it is often difficult to declare the precise classification. Who shall say that the 'Comedy of Errors' is not, in fact, essentially a farce? Or that the Elizabethan tragedy-of-blood is not essentially a melodrama?

Altho the true dramatist cannot but conceive both the incidents of his play and its personages at the same moment, yet we are accustomed to consider tragedy and comedy nobler than melodrama and farce, because in the former the characters themselves seem to create the situations of the plot and to dominate its structure; whereas in the latter it is obvious rather that the situations have evoked the characters, and that these are realized only in so far as the conduct of the story may cause them to reveal the characteristics thus called for. Comedy, then, appears to us as a humorous piece, the action of which is caused by the clash of character on character; and this is a definition which fits the 'Misanthrope,' the 'Marriage of Figaro,' the 'School for Scandal,' and the 'Gendre de M. Poirier.' In all these comedies the plot, the action, the story, is the direct result of the influence of the several characters on one another.

A consideration of the history of dramatic literature will show that comedy of this standard is very infrequent indeed, since the humorous piece is always tending either to stiffen into drama, as in 'Froufrou,' for example, or to relax into farce, as in the 'Rivals.' Satisfactory as the definition seems on the whole, and useful as it is in aiding us to perceive clearly the true limitations of comedy, we must not insist upon applying it too severely or we shall find that we have erased from the list of the writers of comedy the names of two of the greatest masters of stage-humor, Shakspere and Aristophanes, from neither of whom have we a single comic play the action of which is caused solely by the clash of character on character. The delightful fantasies of Shakspere fall into another class, which we may term romantic-comedy, and in which we find the comic plot sustained and set off by a serious plot only artificially adjoined to it. The imaginative exuberance of Aristophanes displayed itself not in any form fairly to be called comedy, but rather in what may be described as lyrical-burlesque.

II

THREE of the most important phases of Greek tragedy are preserved for us in the extant dramas

of Aeschylus, of Sophocles, and of Euripides.
Other tragic writers there were, whose works are
now lost forever; but these three were ever held
to be the foremost, and we are fortunate in having the finest of their plays.   Three phases there
were also in Greek comedy, altho less clearly distinguished; and here we have not been so lucky.
To represent an early stage of its evolution, we
have half a score of the lyrical-burlesques of Aristophanes; but only a single play of his survives
even to suggest to us the kind of comic drama
which was acceptable in a second period when
other humorous playwrights rivaled him.   The
third epoch, illustrated by the noble name of
Menander, can be but guessed at, since we have
not the complete manuscript of even a single play.
Yet an attempt to trace in outline the development of the Greek comic drama is not an altogether impossible task, despite our deficiency in
illustrative examples.

Comedy seems to have sprung into being at
the vintage-festival of the Greek villagers, when
all was jovial gaiety and jesting license in honor
of Dionysus.   "On public occasions," so a recent
historian of the origin of art has reminded us,
"the common mood, whether of joy or sorrow,
is often communicated even to those who were
originally possessed by the opposite feeling; and
so powerful is infection of excitement that a sober
man will join in the antics of his drunken com-

77

rades—yielding to a drunkenness by induction."
And these seasons of contagious revelry were exactly suited to a development of the double desire
of mankind for personation—one man seeking to
get outside of his own individuality and to assume a character not his own, while another finds
his satisfaction rather in the observation of this
simulation, in being a sympathetic spectator when
actions are represented not proper to the actor's
own character.

So it came to pass that there were companies
of young fellows, often disguised grossly as
beasts or birds, who broke out into riotous phallic
dances, enjoyed equally by those who looked on
and by those who took part. In time the dancers
grouped themselves in rival bands, the leaders of
which indulged in a give-and-take of banter and
repartee, certainly vulgar and personal, and probably as direct and artless as the chop-logic dialogs
of the medieval quack-doctor and his jack-pud-
ding, or of the modern ring-master and circus-
clown. The happy improvisation of this carni-
val spirit which happened to delight the crowd
one year would surely be repeated the next year
deliberately, perhaps only to evoke an unexpected
retort with which it would thereafter be conjoined in what might prove to be the nucleus of a
comic scene of some length. Thus a species would
tend to appear, as the tradition was handed

costumes

78

down from season to season, enriching itself constantly with the accretions of every venturesome
jester. However frail this framework might be, it
would be likely to contain a rough realization of
the more obvious types of rural character; and
almost from the beginning there would be abundant and irreverent parody of heroic legend and
of religious myth.

Then in time this inchoate medley of ribald
song and phallic dance and abusive repartee
would come to feel the influence of the other
dramatic species, the origin of which was quite
as humble; it would come to feel the influence of
tragedy as this had been organized at last with its
chorus and its three actors. Indeed, the same
native instinct which led the Greeks to regulate
tragedy and to attach it to a festival of the state
would suggest, sooner or later, that comedy
should also be adopted by the city. And this is
what happened in time, altho Greek comedy,
when taken over by the authorities, was apparently far less advanced and far more archaic than
Greek tragedy had been when first officially regu-
lated. In the earlier dramatic poems of Aeschylus
we perceive tragedy not yet developed out of the
dithyramb and struggling to find its own form;
and so in the earlier comedies of Aristophanes we
discover not only a primitive but a very peculiar
stage of the evolution of the comic drama.

III

CLOSE as Aeschylus, with his dominating chorus, sometimes seems to the earlier rustic lyric, Aristophanes is even closer.   His work is often so formless, his story is sometimes so disconnected, his plot is so carelessly put together, as to force us to the conclusion that the Greeks had not yet perceived the need in the comic drama for that unity which is so striking a characteristic of their greater tragedies.   Owing to this slowness of the Greeks in evolving a type of pure comedy, as they had already evolved a type of pure tragedy, the works of Aristophanes impress us with their strangeness and their inequality.   Aristophanes himself, as we see him in his plays, appears to us in three aspects, each of which is seemingly incompatible with either of the others.

First of all, he is indisputably one of the loftiest lyric poets of Greece, with a surpassing strength of wing for his imaginative flights, and with a surprising sweep of vision when he soars on high.   Secondly, he is the bitterest of satirists, abounding in scorching invective for his political opponents, and never refraining from any violence, any malignity, or any unfair accusation that would help the cause he had at heart.   Thirdly, he is a riotous and exuberant humorist, a forerunner of Rabelais, reveling in sheer fun for its own sake, heartily enjoying every laugh he could call forth from the spectators, and ready at any moment to descend to any depth to evoke it again. It is to his possession of these triple gifts that we may ascribe the variety of opinions held about Aristophanes. The gifts themselves seem incongruous and discordant, and the result of their exercise in a single comic play is sometimes confusing. It is the privilege of great genius, as Voltaire maintained, and, "above all, of a great genius opening a new path, to have great faults."

What seem to us the faults of Aristophanes are partly due to his having opened a new path,—to the fact that comedy, as he understood it, had not yet disentangled itself from the phallic dance out of which it had blossomed. On the modern stage, so we have been told, there are three kinds of dancing, the graceful, the ungraceful, and the disgraceful;—and there need be no doubt as to which adjective can best be applied to the comic chorus of the Greeks. There were not a few lapses into vulgarity on the part of the Attic audiences; and there was at times—as a historian of Greek literature has admitted—"a great deficiency in that elegance and chastity of taste" which we are wont to associate with the name of Athens.

Aristophanes is a lyrist in all his plays, and a satirist also; but only intermittently is he a comic dramatist, concerned especially with the presen-

has come to get the advice of that hero himself. When he has knocked at one of the doors of the dressing-house at the back of the circular orchestra, Heracles (the third actor) comes forth and tells him of the various ways of getting to the nether world. After the demigod has withdrawn, Xanthias complains of the weight of the bundles with which he is burdened. Just then a funeral procession passes before the dressing-house, which formed a low background for the figures in the orchestra; and Dionysus tries in vain to get the bundles carried by the dead man (apparently played by a fourth actor), who refuses the unsatisfactory fee, saying, "I 'd see myself alive first."

Neither in the orchestra itself nor on the front of the dressing-house was there any attempt at scenery, altho by the time of Aristophanes the dressing-house itself may have become a permanent erection, possessing a certain architectural dignity. But the Greek dramatist, tragic or comic, made no effort to realize to the eyes of the spectators the places where the action was supposed to happen; and as he did not particularize, they never gave a thought to mere locality. Thus the Athenian orchestra, like the stage of the Elizabethan theater two thousand years later, was a neutral ground in which actions were exhibited, and which might be here, there, and anywhere, as the plot required. Without any strain on the imagination, the orchestra which had been tacitly accepted as representing an open space in front of the abode of Heracles is immediately thereafter assumed to represent the shores of the Styx. Charon (the third actor again) comes in, rowing his boat,—and if we may snatch a suggestion from modern burlesque, it is quite possible that part of the joke here lay in the obvious make-believe of Charon's skiff, which was perhaps but a bottomless framework hung by a strap from his shoulders as he walked forward, pretending to paddle.

Charon goes to the side of the orchestra where Dionysus and Xanthias are standing, and allows the god to step into his boat, but refuses to take the slave,—who thereupon agrees to rejoin his master by walking around. As Charon puts off with Dionysus, who pretends to help with the rowing, part of the chorus enter, dressed as frogs. These inhabitants of the sunless marsh hoarsely chant a characteristic lyric as Charon and Bacchus propel the boat through the midst of them. Then, as the two voyagers arrive on the other side of the orchestra, the chorus of frogs croaks itself off. Dionysus pays his fare to Charon, who paddles off to the place whence he came,—probably from behind the dressing-house. Dionysus, left alone, calls for Xanthias, who runs

84

around the outer circle of the orchestra to rejoin his master. And when the two are together again the orchestra thereafter is supposed to represent Hades, the under-world.

Scared by the strange specters he now pretends to see, Dionysus appeals for protection to his own priest, whose seat was among the spectators and always in the center of the front row. In this daring unconventionality we may see an anticipation of the modern comedian who leans across the footlights to make fun of the leader of the musicians; just as the attire of Dionysus, doubtfully disguised as Heracles, had elements of humorous incongruity not unlike those observable in the funny man of to-day who wears a high hat when attired in a Roman toga.

Then to the sound of the flute there revels into the orchestra the full chorus, impersonating votaries of Bacchus, happy shades of those who had been duly initiated into the mysteries. While the two visitors look on with humorous comment, the chorus circles in and out with song and dance. In the song a lofty lyric strain is broken into by topical jests, local hits, and personal allusions. In the dance there is a joyous parody of those who took part in the mystic orgies. At last Dionysus gets the chorus to tell him which is the gate of Pluto's realm; and he knocks at one of the doors of the dressing-house, declaring himself to be

Heracles. Then the door flies open and out rushes the gate-keeper, Aeacus (the third actor), who violently berates the sham Heracles for the misdeeds of the real demigod on his visit to Hades. Dionysus recoils in terror, and the gate-keeper goes to summon assistance.

The frightened Dionysus then transfers his lion-skin and club to Xanthias, who is to masquerade as Heracles. But when a maid-servant of Proserpine's (the third actor again) appears to invite Heracles in to a sumptuous banquet, Dionysus insists upon taking back the emblems of the demigod—only once more to yield them up swiftly when two eating-house keepers (the third and fourth actors) assail the false Heracles with bullying demands for damage done on the demigod's previous visit. Then the gate opens again, and Aeacus bids his aids seize the false Heracles, who protests his innocence—and proffers his slave to be tortured in proof of his assertion. Thereupon Dionysus declares himself, but Xanthias maintains his claim, so Aeacus has them flogged alternately to discover which is the god,—he being the one who will not feel the pain of the blows. Altho they cry out, both stand the test so well that the puzzled Aeacus takes them within for Pluto and Proserpine to decide which is truly the god.

The chorus, left alone, turns to the spectators

and becomes the mouthpiece of the satiric dramatist, delivering what is called the *parabasis*, and
what is in fact a personal address of Aristophanes
to his fellow-citizens assembled in the theater, —
an address not unlike our latter-day after-dinner
speech on themes of the hour, now jocularly personal and now raising itself into genuine eloquence. In the modern drama there is nothing
exactly corresponding to the parabasis, altho it is
sometimes like the topical song of a modern
burlesque and sometimes it resembles rather the
prolog of a comedy of Ben Jonson's or Dryden's,
not prefixed to the play, however, but injected
into the middle of it. Like these prologs often,
and like the topical songs generally, the parabasis
had nothing to do with the plot of the play.

When the parabasis is concluded, Aeacus and
Xanthias return, having fraternized as fellow-
servants, delighting to spy on their masters.
The noise of a quarrel is heard; and Aeacus explains that this is Euripides disputing with Aeschylus, whose seat at table he wishes to usurp.
Aeacus further declares that as Dionysus is the
patron of tragedy, Pluto intends to let the newcomer decide the dispute. The two slaves withdraw; and the chorus chants a lyric description
of the coming contest.

Then Dionysus comes back with Aeschylus (the
second actor) and Euripides (the third actor); and

87

we are made to see another characteristic feature
of Aristophanic lyric-burlesque, — the *agon*, the dispute, which has almost the formality of a trial at
law. Aeschylus and Euripides set forth in turn
their views of tragic art, with much satiric distortion of each other's theories, and with much
comic perversion of each other's verses. There
is incessant cut-and-thrust in the dialog, and apparently there is also opportunity for frequent
parody of the actors who had played the parts
from which quotations are made. There is frank
burlesque in the use of scales, by which the best
lines of the opposing poets are weighed in turn;
but Dionysus is still in doubt when Pluto (a fourth
actor) enters to ask for his decision. Unable to
make a choice on literary grounds, Dionysus asks
the advice of the rival dramatists about the contemporary political conditions of Athens; and as
he finds Aeschylus to be the wiser counselor and
the nobler, it is the elder poet that he resolves
to take back with him to earth. Pluto, after
authorizing the departure of Aeschylus, and after
bidding the chorus to escort him triumphantly,
withdraws with Euripides, delaying a moment to
invite Dionysus to remain for a feast. Once more
the chorus circles around; and then, accompanied
by Aeschylus, it trails out of the orchestra.

The 'Frogs' is a delightful example of the
lyrical-burlesque of Aristophanes, commingled of

poetry and of personalities, generous in parody, abundant in fun, and rich in artistic criticism, — but thin in plot and meager in dramatically humorous situations such as later comic dramatists have delighted to devise. It represents an early period of literature, when the several species are as yet imperfectly differentiated; and it is in fact almost as lyric and as satiric as it is dramatic. The story is straggling and the structure is loose. Yet a lyrical-burlesque of this sort was exactly suited to performance at the Dionysiac festival, when the season was held to sanction every conceivable license, and when the people of Athens were so conscious of their freedom that they were ready to laugh at jokes against themselves.

But as soon as the Athenians were shorn of their liberties the play of this type became quite impossible. The tyrants would no longer tolerate it; and perhaps the people would no longer relish it. Personalities were prohibited and satire was pruned. The comic dramatist became cautious and hesitating, and he was forced to seek his theme in private life and not in public affairs. This was fatal to lyrical-burlesque; but it hastened the development of a true comic drama. The plays of Aristophanes were the product of special conditions which have never been repeated, and this is why he stands in a class by himself; he has had no imitators and no followers. Modern comedy owes nothing to his example; and even the comedy of Menander, which was evolved from the comedy of Aristophanes, seems to have speedily become something wholly dissimilar.

IV

THE comedy of Aristophanes was a medley of boisterous comic-opera and of lofty lyric poetry, of vulgar ballet and of patriotic oratory, of indecent farce and of pungent political satire, of acrobatic pantomime and of brilliant literary criticism, of cheap burlesque and of daringly imaginative fantasy. Obviously most of these elements have no necessary relation to the drama, and one by one they were eliminated. The political personalities had to go first; then the lyric poetry and the imaginative fantasy. The 'Plutus' of Aristophanes himself seems to be a specimen of this uncertain transition stage, in which the humorous poet is sadly shorn of his exuberance. He is not content to deal with the commonplaces of every-day life; and the theme he treats is really a fable, or rather an apolog. Yet in 'Plutus' the absence of the more extravagant elements of his lyrical-burlesques brings the later play closer to comedy as we now understand it than were the earlier pieces.

In the course of a few years after Aristophanes,

Greek comedy still further simplified itself. It gave up the parabasis, always an undramatic excrescence; and it surrendered the chorus, thus abandoning at once the ballet and the opera. It made up for the loss of these things by elaborating the more dramatic elements, by relying more upon the delineation of character, and by giving more thought to the building up of the plot and to the invention of comic situations. It responded also to the influence of the more realistic treatment of life which Euripides had introduced into tragedy. Indeed, it is quite possible that there was a fairly close agreement in method and in attitude between Euripides, the last of the great writers of Greek tragedy, and Menander, the first of the great writers of Greek comedy.

In the plays of Aeschylus, we see the lyric and the dramatic existing side by side, and the drama has not succeeded in making the song subservient. In the plays of Sophocles, we find the lyric fused with the dramatic, welded into it, made helpful to the tragic story. In the plays of Euripides, we discover that the chorus lingers, like an atrophied organ which the dramatist dared not amputate out of regard for tradition. In the plays of Menander, we note that the needful operation has taken place. At the hands of Euripides the chorus serves only to fill out the lyric interludes of the dramatic action; and it is this *entr'acte* music that Menander omits. Greek tragedy had been lyric in its origin, and was perforce poetic; whereas Greek comedy, after Aristophanes, was free to be prosaic, as was needful in dealing more directly with the facts of every-day existence. As De Quincey says, it is ever "the acknowledged duty of comedy to fathom the coynesses of human nature, and to arrest the fleeting phenomena of human demeanor."

Unfortunately for us, no play of Menander's has survived. We have a few fragments of scenes; we have many quoted sentences; we have the Latin adaptations of Plautus and Terence: but we have not a single play complete, by which we could make up our own minds as to his dramaturgic skill. We can judge of him as a poet and as a moralist by means of the lines preserved here and there by his admirers. But altho we have one play of Terence's which seems to have been derived without admixture from Menander, this is really not enough to justify any judgment as to his play-making faculty. We do not know much more about Menander as a dramatist than we should know about Shakspere as a dramatist, if his works were altogether lost, and if all we had left were, first, the librettos of the French operas which had been founded on his plots, and, second, the extracts in some dictionary of 'Familiar Quotations.' We are at liberty to guess that Menander found compensation for his sinking from the lyric heights of Aristophanes by not descending to the depths of base vulgarity in which the earlier poet reveled. We may surmise that his plays were often genuine comedies rather than mere farces,—in that he sought the truth of life itself rather than the boisterous laughter evoked by exaggeration. Certainly his contemporaries continually testify to the veracity of his scenes. "On the stage," as Chamfort declared, "the aim is effect; but the difference between the good dramatist and the bad is that the former seeks effect by reasonable means, while for the latter any and all means are excellent."

In other words, the plays of Menander seem to have been an anticipation of the modern comedy-of-intrigue and the modern comedy-of-manners. The plots were ingenious and plausible, and they were peopled with characters common in Athens at that time;—the miserly father, the spendthrift son, the intriguing servant, the braggart soldier, the obsequious parasite, the woman of pleasure, —and here in this last type we find the most marked difference between Menander and Molière, for example. In modern comedy, as in modern society, women occupy many conspicuous positions; but in Athens respectable women took no part in social life, remaining at home and caring for their households. In Greek comedy, therefore, women are little seen, and those who do appear belong to the less respectable classes. It was impossible for Menander to treat such a theme as served Molière in the 'Femmes Savantes,' Sandeau in 'Mademoiselle de la Seiglière,' and Ibsen in the 'Doll's Home'; and here, no doubt, is the most serious limitation of Greek comedy. To Menander himself the deprivation is most injurious, since he obviously possessed the delicacy of perception that would have enabled him to handle feminine character with insight and subtlety. His prevailing tone, as Professor Jebb notes, is "that of polite conversation, not without passages of tender sentiment, grave thought, or almost tragic pathos."

Altho the chorus had disappeared in Menander's day, the tradition of the mask still survived. The mask was probably a pasteboard head not unlike those now seen in our comic pantomimes; and a great variety of them had been modeled for use in comedy, each of which served to declare at once the character of the wearer and to announce on his first appearance whether, for instance, he was a dutiful young man or a wanton prodigal. Indeed, there were said to be ten distinct masks available for the several young men of the play, nine for the old men, and seven for the slaves. In a theater so vast as that at Athens,

it would have been impossible for the spectators
to perceive the changing expression and the
mobility of feature which on the modern stage
add so much to our enjoyment.   Probably, moreover, the Athenian of old was no more annoyed
by the facial rigidity of the masked characters
than our children to-day are disturbed by the
unchanging countenances of Mr. Punch and Mrs.
Judy and of Mr. Punch's other wooden-headed
friends.

V

THE Greeks were clever and witty; they were
admirably qualified for comedy; and their language was likewise easy and flexible.   The
Romans who conquered them and who fell captive to their charm were a more serious people,
not so likely to appreciate the comic drama; and
their language was a lapidary tongue, grave and
concise and a little lacking in lightness and fluid-
ity.   Latin reflects perfectly the sanity, the solidity, the robust common sense, of the race that
spoke it.   Altho there was always a certain austerity among the Romans, a certain deficiency in
humor, they had early shown their appreciation
of the primitive comic play which had been developed by their neighbors, the Etrurians.   These
Atellan fables seem to have been little better than
crude farces, not unlike the rough rustic plays of

the Grecian vintage-festivals out of which Greek comedy had been evolved. The themes of these little pieces were probably as vulgar as the fragments of dialog that have been preserved; and the chief characters were broadly marked rural types, the memory of which may have survived through the empire and through the middle ages to emerge again in certain of the personages of the Italian comedy-of-masks.

However low in language these early attempts might be, and however rude in art, they could have served as a root out of which a genuine Latin comedy might have been developed, if the Romans had really wanted such a thing. But before this coarse Italic humor had a chance to raise itself into literature, it was thrust aside, and its place was taken by Latin adaptations of Greek comedy. The native comic drama that had proved its power to please the populace did not die of this neglect,—indeed, it seems to have had a sturdy vitality; but it was deprived of the chance of artistic development, and no specimens of it have been preserved. It survived humbly in the shadow of its important Greek rival; and yet, long after all traces of the Latin perversion of the Attic drama had disappeared, the coarser Oscan play showed signs of existence in the nooks and corners of the peninsula. Being unliterary, a drama of this primitive type rarely gets itself

recorded, even tho it continues to please the uncultivated public.

The earlier Roman attitude toward the arts had
been a little contemptuous; but this changed
when they began to apprehend the beauty of
Greek civilization. Having discovered that Greek
culture was valuable, the Romans, being a practical people, proceeded at once to import it,
wholesale, and in the original package. Their
dramatists became adapters, taking the plots of
the plays of Menander and of Menander's clever
contemporaries, and transferring these into Latin,
leaving the scene in Athens, but inserting an
abundance of local allusions to Roman manners.
They kept the types of character which the
Athenian dramatist had observed and which often
had only rare counterparts in Rome; the braggart
coward, for example, was a Greek and not a
Roman,—the Greek had no stomach for fighting,
whereas the Roman had shortened his sword
and enlarged his boundaries. As a result this
Latin comic drama is singularly unreal,—as unreal
as certain English adaptations from the French
and the German, in which we feel a blank incongruity between the foreign code of manners on
which the story is conditioned and the supposedly
Anglo-Saxon characters by which it has to be
carried out.

Nor was this the sole disadvantage under which

Latin comedy labored, for the circumstances of its performance were also disastrous. Plays were provided regularly three times a year by the city authorities, and also at irregular intervals when a high functionary took office or when a great dignitary died. The actors were often slaves, who might expect a beating if they failed to be applauded, and who might hope for their freedom if they succeeded in pleasing the public. The performances took place in huge theaters modeled upon that in Athens, except that two important changes were made: the orchestra, being no longer needed for the dance of the chorus, was reserved for the seats of the more important officials,—and therefore, in order that these spectators might see, the dressing-house was lowered and brought forward, so that its roof might serve as a stage. But of these officials and of the members of the upper circles there were few likely often to be present; and owing to this absence of the more cultivated public, a Roman audience did not represent all classes of the community like the Athenian audience—and like the London and Parisian audiences to which Shakspere and Molière were to appeal.

The audience which the Latin dramatist had to try to please was the roughest and most stubborn of any known to the history of the theater. It contained chiefly men of the lower orders—and very few of these were natives, for the Roman was serving abroad as a soldier or settled as a colonist, while his city was filled with a riffraff of rustics and strangers, uncouth barbarians many of them, prisoners of war, and freedmen, ignorant and brutal, knowing just enough Latin to make it serve as a *lingua franca*. Any delicacy would be wasted on a crowd like this; and no jest could be too gross or too violent to amuse coarse creatures whose chief joy had been in the bloody sports of the arena. Sometimes Gresham's law seems as imperative in the drama as in finance; the lower tends to drive out the higher,—at least, we all know that the theaters of New York have a barren fortnight when a huge circus comes to town. It is no wonder Terence complained that one of his plays was twice deserted by the spectators, who were suddenly tempted away by the report of more violent delights elsewhere.

VI

BEFORE a mob of this sort, the Latin dramatist sought especially to make his plot clear, and he was afraid of no reiteration to avoid misunderstanding. He could not count on any intelligence of comprehension, and so we find at the beginning of one of his plays a prolog in which is set forth the exact situation at the opening of the story, and which then proceeds to tell in advance what the plot was going to be, returning finally to explain again the state of affairs at the moment when the action was to open. It is doubtful whether all the prologs as we have them are the work of Plautus himself; and it is true that this explanation may have been distended simply to allow more time for the turbulent folk still standing to find seats, or at least to settle themselves in their places. But even if the prolog is thus made to serve as a substitute for the overture of the modern theater, there is something pitiful in the precise prolixity of Plautus, so afraid that the most stupid may fail to catch some essential point. Yet the attitude of the Roman dramatist is only an exaggeration of that recommended by the old London stage-manager who said that if you want the British public to understand anything, you must tell them you are going to do it, next you must tell them you are doing it, and at last you must tell them you have done it,—" and then, confound 'em, perhaps they'll understand you!"

The stage was a mere strip of platform in front of a wide architectural background. In the later Roman theaters, in that of Orange for instance, this rear wall had become a stately elevation with three elaborate doorways and with decorative statuary. But even in the time of Plautus this background, altho only a temporary erection of wood, contained doors which served to designate the homes of certain of the characters. In the 'Captives,' for example, the speaker of the prolog tells the spectators explicitly that a father who has lost his son dwells in the house on the right, and that another father who has also lost his son lives in the house on the left; and two of the doors in the rear wall were sufficient to represent these two domiciles.

The actors did not wear masks. Many of their speeches were accompanied by a soloist on the flute. Some of these passages were declaimed to this accompaniment, thus resembling the recitative of modern opera; and some were actually sung to set tunes. Indeed, we are told that sometimes a singer came forward to the side of the actor to deliver these lyrical passages while the comedian merely made the appropriate gestures, —a convention which seems to us monstrous, but which in itself is perhaps no more absurd than the full orchestra accompanying the song of Amiens far in the depths of the Forest of Arden.

The first duty of the Roman dramatist was to be so clear that the stupid spectators could not fail to follow the successive situations; and his second obligation, even more difficult, was to move to mirth his miscellaneous and uneducated audience. Altho in theory Roman comedy was

only Greek comedy written in Latin, and altho
Roman comedy was therefore supposed to deal
with Athenian life and manners, as a matter of
fact the Latin dramatists managed to get into
their plays not a little of the local color of their
own city. Plautus especially, not knowing himself much about Athenian life and manners, and
well aware that his uncultivated Roman audience
knew still less and cared nothing at all,—Plautus
dealt very freely with his Greek original.

The scene of his plays is always supposed to
be in Athens, but Plautus continually draws on
his own intimate knowledge of the Roman populace. He had a thorough acquaintance with the
speech, the methods, the every-day actions, of the
very class from which was collected the audience
to which he appealed. It was his object to make
this audience laugh, and he could do it by showing them as they lived, by local allusions, by a
humorous reproduction of their sayings and their
doings. Plautus no more tries deliberately to
mirror Athenian habits and deeds than Shakspere
—in giving us Dogberry and Verges—tried to
mirror the ways of speech and the judicial customs
of Sicily. In spite of his professed Greek original,
Plautus was really giving a picture of low life in
Rome, as broadly humorous and as fundamentally
veracious as the picture of low life in New York
which was visible in Mr. Harrigan's comic

dramas, such as 'Squatter Sovereignty' for example.

Here Plautus was apparently availing himself of the direct methods of the earlier native comedy of the Italians, of the Atellan fables, and of Fescennine satire; and this is just what a born dramatist would do instinctively, even tho he had to follow a foreign plot. There is no denying that Plautus was a born dramatist, — born out of time, unfortunately, and fallen upon evil days. The circumstances of the theater did not encourage or even permit his full development. But even if he was taking over his plot from Menander, he was strikingly fresh in his sketches of life among the lowly as he knew it in Rome. He was vulgar, no doubt, but vulgarity was perhaps what his rude audience most relished; and altho frank and plain-spoken, he was not as indecorous as Aristophanes, and he was never so indecent as Wycherley. He had a hearty gaiety as well as a broad humor; indeed, in comic force, in *vis comica*, in the sheer power of compelling laughter, he can withstand a comparison even with Molière, the greatest of all comic dramatists.

VII

THIS comic force is just what was lacking in Terence. Where Plautus was plebeian in his point of view, Terence was patrician. Plautus was a practical playwright, and Terence was a cultivated man-of-letters. Plautus was invaluable for the information he has indirectly given us about the life of the Roman populace; Terence was valuable chiefly because his scholarly translations have preserved for us not a few of the best of Menander's comedies. Plautus dealt freely with the works of the Greek dramatists, knowing that his audience was eager to be amused by bold buffoonery, while Terence sought to give a high literary polish to his faithful renderings of Greek plays of a graceful elegance, altho he knew they were to be acted before spectators incapable of appreciating either elegance or grace. It is no wonder that the comedies of the later writer failed; he lacked the instinct of the born dramatist, who cannot help feeling the pulse of his contemporaries and responding to their unspoken demands. Terence had to wait for a fit audience until his plays were performed in the Italian Renascence before an assembly of cultivated scholars, abundantly capable of appreciating his refinement.

It has been suggested that there was in Menander something of the well-bred ease of the man of the world, such as we see it in Thackeray, and that in Terence there is rather the terseness and high finish of Congreve. Certainly Terence is like Congreve in that he was of importance

rather as a man-of-letters than as a dramatist.
He was essentially a stylist, concerned rather with
his manner than with his matter. Indeed, as his
comedies dealt with the life of Athens, which he
did not know at first hand, and not with the life
of Rome, which he could not help knowing, and
in the language of which he was writing, he cannot be acquitted of unreality and artificiality. He
had at times a haughty melancholy of his own;
and he resented the stupidity of the public, incapable of seeing the surpassing merit of his transparent translations. But he had no roots in the
soil; he was not only content to be an imitator:
he was even proud of being second-hand; and
what he strove for was at best but a reflected
glory. This was indeed the fatal defect of the Latin
drama,—that the Romans were satisfied with a
colonial attitude in all matters of art. They had
conquered the Greeks politically; but the Greeks
had taken them captive intellectually. Instead of
developing the native drama, and elevating it into
literature by giving it form and substance, they
preferred to dwell in servile deference to the
greater Greeks.

A dramatic literature is necessarily conditioned
by the audience for which it is intended. A mob
of lewd fellows of the baser sort will demand
plays fitted to their low likings; and this is one
reason why the Romans, with all their ability,

failed to have a worthy ramatic literature—their theater was abandoned to the vulgar. On the other hand, there is danger also if the dramatist is forced to please only the cultivated, who are ever prone to apply personal and dilettante standards; and it is this which accounts for the sterility of the Weimar theater when it was controlled by Goethe. But in the Elizabethan theater, altho the rude and boisterous groundlings filled the yard, there were city madams in the rooms above, and there were gallants sitting on the stage itself; and altogether the playwright had before him a representative public. So Molière, inventing certain of his comedies for the court of the king, always counted on bringing them out later in his own theater for the joy of the burghers of Paris. Yet it may be doubted whether any audience to be found in Paris under Louis XIV, or in London under Elizabeth, was as carefully trained to understand and to appreciate, or was as delicately discriminating in its taste, as those which in Athens flocked to behold the tragedies of Sophocles and the comedies of Menander.

IV. THE MEDIEVAL DRAMA

I

THE Greeks, from the rudest beginnings, and by the aid of their incomparable instinct for form, brought to perfection a lofty type of tragedy and an original kind of comedy. The Latins, who had at least the germ of a comic drama of their own, were proud to borrow the comedy of the Greeks, altho in their hands it could not but be sadly sterile. In the stalwart days of the Roman commonwealth the drama seems to have had scant encouragement in the capital, either from the men of culture or from the coarser populace. When at last the empire solidified itself upon the ruins of the republic, and the eagles of Rome were borne almost to the confines of the world, the cosmopolitan inhabitants of this immense realm were never educated to appreciate the calm pleasures of the theater. They were encouraged to prefer the fierce joy of the chariot-race, the brutal delight of the arena, and the poignant ecstasy of the gladiatorial combat. The sole vestiges of the true drama were the vulgar farces of the rustics that lingered in odd corners of Italy, and the obscene and cruel pantomimes which were devised to gratify the relish of the mob for lewdness and to glut its liking for gore. Neither the rough comic plays of the peasants nor the abominable pantomimes of the court had any relation to literature.

After the conversion of Constantine, the lustful and bloody spectacles were accurst by the church. It was to be expected that the Fathers should condemn the theater absolutely, since it was—in the sole aspect in which they had occasion to behold it—unspeakably vile. With the triumph of Christianity theatrical performances were abolished; and it must have seemed as tho the drama was destroyed forever. It is true that in some obscure nooks rural farces might linger, forgotten links in the chain that was to stretch from the Atellan fables to the late Italian comedy-of-masks. But this doubtful survival seems to have little significance, and apparently the break in the tradition of the theater was final and irreparable. When Constantinople supplanted Rome as the capital of civilization, dramatic literature, which had been a chief glory of Athens, ceased from off the earth. For a thousand years and more the history of the drama is all darkness and vacancy; and we have not a single name recorded of any author writing plays to be performed by actors, in a theater, before an audience.

The desire for the drama, which seems to be instinctive in human nature the wide world over, from the Aleutian Islanders to the Bushmen of Australia, the impulse to personate and to take pleasure in beholding a story set forth in action, —this may have been dormant during the long centuries, or it may have found some means of gratifying itself unrecorded in the correspondence of the time or by the chroniclers.   Acrobats there were, and wandering minstrels; and now and again we catch glimpses of singers of comic songs and of roving amusers who entertained with feats of sleight-of-hand, or who exhibited trained animals. These performers, always pop- ular with the public at large, were also called in upon occasion to enliven the solid feasts of the rulers. Gibbon records that at the supper-table of Theodoric, in the middle of the fifth century, buffoons and performers of pantomimes were "sometimes introduced to divert, not to offend, the company by their ridiculous wit."   And Froissart records that when he was a guest at the court of Gaston Phébus, toward the end of the fourteenth century, strolling jesters sometimes presented a little play during the repast, or acro- bats went through their daring performances. The entertainments described by Gibbon and by

Froissart, however long the interval between them, bear an obvious likeness to our latter-day "vaudeville suppers."

But none the less dramatic literature, which had flourished so gloriously in Greece, and which had tried to establish itself in Italy, was dead at last; and even the memory of it seems to have departed, for, in so far as the works of the Attic tragedians and of the Roman comedians were known at all, they were thought of rather as poetry to be read than as plays that had been acted. The art of acting was a lost art, and the theaters themselves fell into ruin. So it was that when the prejudice against the drama wore itself out in time, and when the inherent demand for the pleasure which only the theater can give became at last insistent, there was to be seen the spontaneous evolution of a new form, fitted specially to satisfy the needs of the people under the new circumstances. This new drama of the middle ages sprang into being wholly uninfluenced by the drama of the Greeks; it was, indeed, as free a growth as the Attic drama itself had been.

In its origin again, the medieval drama was not unlike the drama of the Greeks, —in that the germ of it was religious, and that it was slowly elaborated from what was at first only a casual accompaniment of public worship. The new form had its birth actually at the base of the altar and at the foot of the pulpit; and it was fostered by the Christian church, the very organization that had cursed the old form when that was decadent and corrupted. Coming into being as an illustrative incident of the service on certain special days of the ecclesiastical year, the drama grew sturdily within the walls of the church until it was strong enough to support itself; and when at last it ventured outside, it remained for a long while religious in intent. The history of its development is very much the same throughout Europe; and the religious drama of England is very like that of France (from which, indeed, it is in some measure derived), just as the religious drama of Italy is like that of Spain, altho neither of these had any appreciable influence on the other.

The reason for this uniformity is obvious enough. It was due to the double unity of the medieval world,—that which resulted from possession of the same religion and that which was caused by the consciousness of a former union under the rule of Rome. All the peoples of western Europe had inherited the same customs and the same traditions, because they had all been included in the Roman Empire, which had stretched itself from the Black Sea to the Atlantic. When, at last, the vigor of the Roman government was relaxed, the barbarians of the north had broken in,

and had swept through southern Europe into
Africa and into Asia.   The Franks had taken Gaul
for their own, the Goths had repopulated Italy,
and the Vandals had traversed Spain; and as they
had all of them accepted Christianity, sooner or
later, the most distant lands had once more come
under the sway of Rome.

This is why it is that we find in the middle
ages a unity of western and southern Europe
closer than ever before or ever since.   Just before
the Renascence, the peoples of all these varied
stocks, however much they might differ individu-
ally, were bound together by the common use of
the Latin language and by the common dominion
of the Roman law; they held the same beliefs
and they yielded to the same superstitions; they
revered the same ideals, they acted on the same
theories, and they had very much the same habits.
As yet the idea of nationality had not been born;
and the solidarity of those speaking each of the
modern languages had not been suggested.   Europe was a unit because, altho it was segregated
into towns and even into small provinces, these
had not yet been compacted into distinct nations.
Towns and provinces and kingdoms were all in
accord in accepting the supremacy of the pontiff
of Rome and in yielding a doubtful allegiance to
the head of the shadowy monarchy which was
still called the Holy Roman Empire.

II

To declare with certainty just where it was that the new drama first gave sign of life is quite impossible; and it is equally impossible to decide whether it sprang up of its own accord in half a dozen different places, or whether the first tempting suggestion of it was carried abroad from the church of its origin for adoption in churches widely scattered. There was far more migration in the middle ages than is admitted by those who consider them merely as a long period of stagnation. Priests and merchants were continually passing from one city to another a thousand miles distant; and as the most of Europe was included in the Holy Roman Empire, and as it acknowledged also the sway of the Roman Pope, men could remove from the east to the west, and from the south to the north, with no feeling that they were relinquishing their nationality, especially as the priests, at least, could make themselves understood everywhere in the same tongue.

Latin was the language of the church and of its liturgy; and it is out of the Latin liturgy of the Christian church that the drama of the modern European languages has been slowly developed. It is not possible to trace all the steps by which a very brief semi-dramatic adjunct of the service of certain special days of the ecclesiastical year was slowly elaborated into a more or less complete dramatic scene; and it is difficult to declare just how it was that these several scenes were in time detached from the liturgy and combined together in a cycle which presented the chief events of the gospel-story. But it is practicable to prove that there was a steady growth, beginning with a single brief scene acted within the church, by the priests, in Latin, and almost as part of the liturgy, and developing, in the course of time, into a sequence of scenes, acted by laymen outside the church, in the vernacular, and wholly disconnected from the service.

The Christian church had so arranged its calendar that every one of the chief events in the career of Jesus was regularly commemorated in the course of the year. Its liturgy was rich in symbolism; and as the ritual was not everywhere uniform, opportunites were frequent for suggestive variations devised by the devout priests, who were diligently seeking the means by which they could best bring home the central truths of religion to a very ignorant congregation. In many churches, for example, the crucifix was removed from the altar on Good Friday and borne to a receptacle supposed to represent the sepulcher, whence it was taken on Easter morning to be restored solemnly to the altar, in testimony of the Resurrection.

The gospel-story is rarely pure narrative; as it is to be expected in the accounts of eye-witnesses, it abounds in actual dialog. And where a dramatic passage was included in the service nothing was easier or more natural than to let the narrative be read by the officiating priest, while assigning the actual dialog to other priests, each of whom should deliver the speeches of a single character. Thus on Easter morning, in the colloquy between Saints Peter and John and the three Marys, when the apostles ask what had been seen at the sepulcher, each of the three Marys can answer in turn. In time this interchange of dialog would lend itself to amplification; and there is preserved a Latin manuscript in which the scene at the sepulcher was presented both in dialog and in action. In this interpolation into the Easter service, the three Marys, Saint Peter and Saint John, and "One in the likeness of a gardener," all impersonated by priests or choirboys, speak the words set down for them in the sacred text, and do whatever is there recorded of them.

Altho scenes of this sort seem to have been first invented to embellish the Easter services, Christmas was soon discovered to offer an equal opportunity. For example, one of the very earliest of these enlargements of the ritual showed the quest of the shepherds. At the proper moment certain

priests holding crooks in their hands are to be
seen standing in the transept, and a chorister
from a gallery above announces to them the glad
tidings of the birth of Christ, the Savior of men.
Then, while other choristers scattered throughout
the galleries sing, "Glory to God in the highest,
and on earth peace, good will to men," the Shepherds advance to the choir, and halt at length before
a manger which has been arranged near the altar
and by the side of an image of the Virgin Mary.
There two other priests, personating Women
who had aided the Virgin-mother, ask the Shepherds what it is they are seeking, and then display
the infant Jesus to them. The Shepherds, after
adoring the new-born babe and its mother, depart singing "For unto us a child is born,"—
which is the beginning of the high mass regularly
celebrated at Christmas.

More elaborate is a liturgical embellishment
dealing with the Three Kings, the Three Wise
Men of the East, and calling for a greater variety
of characters and for a more obvious effort to indicate the different localities where the several
portions of the gospel-story were supposed to take
place. The huge churches, which had begun to
spring up all over Europe in the century following the fateful year 1000, were not encumbered
with pews, as are our smaller modern edifices;
and their free floor-space would contain multi-

Herod, silent on his throne all this time, has been supposed not to see the Shepherds; but the Kings he does see, and so he sends a Messenger to ask who they are. The Messenger questions them at length, and finally bears back to Herod the dread news that the King of Kings has been born, and that the Three Wise Men of the East are being guided to his cradle by the star above their heads. Herod then consults the Scribes, who proceed to search the Scriptures and to inform him that the promised Redeemer should be born in Bethlehem. Herod rages violently at these ill tidings, and knocks the books from the hands of the Scribes; but, pacified by his son, he bids the Three Wise Men follow the star and find the newborn King, commanding them on their return to let him know where the royal infant lay. Herod and all his courtiers then become silent again, and cease to take part in the play until they shall be once more needed. The Three Kings, bearing their gifts and led by the star, advance toward the altar and meet the Shepherds, who now come into the action again. The Shepherds sing a hymn of praise; and the Three Kings ask them what they have seen. The Shepherds, after declaring that they have beheld the holy child lying in a manger, withdraw; and the Three Kings follow the star to the altar, where the two Women ask them who they are and what they are seeking.

The Three Wise Men reveal the object of their journeying; and the babe is then displayed to them.   They adore it, presenting their gifts of gold and frankincense and myrrh.   The Angel in the pulpit or gallery above them breaks in, declaring that the prophecies are fulfilled, and bidding the Three Kings go home by another way. Thereupon the Wise Men, chanting a hymn of praise, pass through the assembled multitude and leave the church by a western door.   Herod is supposed not to see them take their leave, but just as soon as they are gone, the Messenger informs the monarch that they have departed in disobedience; thereupon Herod draws his sword and gives it to a Soldier, bidding him go forth and slay all the children.

Here the play seems to end, altho, as we have also the manuscript of a representation of the Flight into Egypt and of the Slaughter of the Innocents, it is probable that, in some churches, on some occasions, all the various incidents connected with the Nativity were set forth in action, one after the other.   What it is most important for us to seize and to fix in our memories is that these episodes of the gospel-story—the Scene of the Shepherds, the Adoration of the Wise Men, the Wrath of Herod, the Slaughter of the Innocents—came into existence each by itself, having been put into dramatic form as a more vivid and impressive illustration of the liturgy; and that possibly a long while elapsed before any one thought to combine these scattered scenes into a sequence. But after the Christmas cycle of the Nativity had knit itself together, following or preceding a similar Easter cycle of the separate scenes of the Crucifixion and the Resurrection, it was probably not very long before an attempt was made to link the two cycles together, filling out the gaps by dramatizing the more interesting of the intervening episodes of the gospel-story,—the Raising of Lazarus, for instance, and the Driving of the Money-changers from the Temple. Thus the whole story of the life and death and resurrection of Jesus could be presented in dialog in the church by the priests themselves, in Latin, and as part of the service, for the enlightenment of the ignorant population in those dark ages.

Altho the priests who put it together had not given a thought to this aspect of it, the story of Jesus is truly dramatic, not only in its humanity, in its color, in its variety, in its infinite pathos, but also and chiefly in its full possession of the prime essential of a true drama—in its having at the heart of it a struggle, an exhibition of determination, a clash of contending desires. Indeed, it is the most dramatic of all struggles, for it is the perpetual conflict of good and evil. To us moderns the issue is sharply joined; but in the medieval church it was even more obvious, since in the middle ages no one ever doubted that a personal Devil was forever striving to thwart the will of a personal God. In the passion-play, which showed in action all the leading events of the life of Christ, both of the contestants were set boldly before the spectators—God himself high in Heaven, and the Devil escaping from Hell-mouth to work his evil will among mankind.

After all these little scenes, each of them devised originally for the special day of the church calendar when the event was commemorated, had been combined into a New Testament cycle, and after there had been prefixed to it certain episodes dramatized from the Old Testament also, and selected because they seemed to prefigure the gospel-story,—after the passion-play had become a mystery, and after it was thus grown to its full length and swollen huge, it was found to be too unwieldy for presentation in the church itself, and too burdensome for the clergy to perform. Thrust out of the church, it may have lingered for a while in the churchyard or in the cloisters or in the great square before the sacred edifice. As the successive episodes of the gospel-story no longer had an intimate connection with the actual liturgy, the tendency was increased to substitute for the Latin of the priests the language of popular taste, and it had taken over more than one of the accepted devices of the primitive comic plays, such as the strolling buffoons were wont to perform. The brief farces of these wandering minstrels may have been mere dramatized anecdotes, practical jokes in dialog, pantomimic horse-play of an elementary type; they were wholly unliterary, and being often even unwritten, they have rarely been preserved. Yet it is perfectly possible that this medieval farce, with its hearty fun and its frankness of speech, is the direct descendant of the rude humor of the Latin rustics, surviving unobserved and neglected through all the centuries of the dark ages, and serving humbly to satisfy, in some measure, the perpetual human desire for a story told in action. When at last the serious play had been developed out of the services of the church, this folk-drama was ready to supply the comic element, without which any representation of life must needs be one-sided.

Fortunately chance has saved for our enlightenment not a few of the later specimens of this folk-play; and we can see that it was generally as unliterary and as inartistic as one might expect, and that it assumed a great variety of forms. It might be merely a burlesque-sermon satirizing the clergy or the civil authorities; it might be a monolog in which, for example, a boastful character unwillingly admitted his own unworthiness; it might be little more than a comic song with a telling refrain and with illustrative gestures; it might be a dialog of cut-and-thrust repartee not unlike the pungent talk interchanged by the ring-master and the clown in the modern circus; it might even be a lively little play with a simple ingenuity of situation, presenting a scene of every-day life with an abundance of pertinent detail.

Such, for example, is the French farce of the 'Tub,' with its three characters of the Husband, the Wife, and the Mother-in-law.   The Husband is henpecked; and the Wife, aided by the Mother-in-law, has even gone so far as to draw up an agreement for the Husband to sign, in which he has bound himself to do all the work of the household, and in which his several duties are specified, item by item.   Then, as it happens, the Wife falls into the tub in which they have been washing the household linen, and she cries to the Husband to help her out.   He consults the agreement, and then refuses to assist her, as that is not set down in writing.   The Wife insists; and the Husband protests that he is willing to do all that he has agreed to do, but nothing more. The Mother-in-law intervenes, but she cannot extricate the Wife without the Husband's help; and he refers her again to the document.   He is ready

to bake and to boil and to get up early to make
the fire, as he has promised to do; but as for pull-
ing the Wife out of the tub, that is not his duty,
since it is not down in the bond.   The Wife and
the Mother-in-law scold and threaten at first; but
at last they appeal.   The Husband suggests that
if he is to do more than he has bound himself to
do in writing, then the agreement is really useless, and he proposes that it shall be torn up before he rescues the Wife.   As her danger is now
pressing, the two women agree to this; the bond
is rent in twain, and the Husband extricates the
Wife from the tub.   The household is once more
upon a peace footing; and yet the Husband,
warned by experience, remarks to the spectators
that he wonders how long it will last.

This little farce of the 'Tub' is French; but
it has its analogs in the other modern literatures.
It has a certain likeness to the dispute between
Noah and his Wife in an English mystery—a very
amusing scene, indeed, in which the spouse of
the patriarch refuses to enter the ark unless she
can bring her friends with her, and in which,
when she is taken on board by force, she gives
her venerable husband a sound box on the ear.

French, also, is the farce of 'Master Peter
Patelin,' by far the most artistic of all the medieval comic plays.   Patelin is a swindling lawyer
who is in the depths of poverty.   He goes to a

Draper and wheedles him out of six yards of
woolen cloth; and when the Draper comes to him
for payment, Patelin is in bed, and his Wife protests that he has not been out of the house for
weeks. The Draper is almost persuaded that he
is the victim of hallucination, and he returns to
his shop to see if he has truly lost the cloth.
Finding that it is really gone, he rushes again to
Patelin's lodging, whereupon the lawyer pretends
to be mad, and overwhelms the unfortunate
tradesman with a flood of words, first in one of
the French dialects, and then in those of another,
until at last the Draper withdraws, half believing
that it is the devil who has played a trick on him.
Then there comes to Patelin the Shepherd of the
Draper, whom his master is suing for having
stolen some sheep, and the Shepherd engages the
lawyer to defend him.   Patelin bids the Shepherd to pretend to be foolish and no matter what
question the Judge may put to him, to answer
only with the bleat of a lamb, — " Baa-a!"   When
the trial comes up before the Judge, Patelin hides
himself behind the Shepherd so that the Draper
shall not see him.   But the shopkeeper does
catch sight of the lawyer at last, and he instantly
demands payment for his cloth, to the complete
astonishment of the Judge, who had supposed
that he was trying the Shepherd for sheep-steal-
ing.   The Draper gets confused also, and accuses

the Shepherd of stealing the cloth and the lawyer of taking the sheep. The puzzled Judge questions the Shepherd, who answers no word but " Baa-a!" and Patelin adroitly pleads that the poor fellow is plainly an idiot. The Draper continues to insist on payment for his cloth, altho the Judge in vain begs him to come back to his sheep. In the end, the magistrate has to acquit the Shepherd for lack of evidence against him. Then the wretched Draper asks Patelin if he is not the lawyer who had been seen in bed only a few minutes before; and Patelin daringly bids him go to the house and look for himself. When the tortured tradesman has departed, Patelin turns to the Shepherd and demands his fee for getting the man off from the charge against him. And now are the tables turned: the biter is bit, and the swindler is swindled; for the Shepherd simply answers, "Baa-a!" The play comes to an end swiftly with the discomfited Patelin trying vainly to catch his deceitful client.

'Master Peter Patelin' is a French farce, to be acted by itself whenever a company of strollers happened to have five performers; but it is curiously like one of the Nativity scenes in an English mystery. When the Shepherds are watching their flocks by night, a neighbor joins them—one Mak, a man of evil repute. To keep him under guard when they go to sleep, the Shepherds make Mak lie down between them. But the precaution is unavailing, as Mak gets up, and steals a lamb, and takes it to his Wife, and then returns to his place. When the Shepherds wake, there is Mak between them; but a lamb is missing. Mak is suspected at once, and the Shepherds go to his house, where Mak's Wife has the lamb swaddled in a cradle like a babe. The Shepherds search everywhere and find nothing, until one of them goes to the cradle and remarks that the babe has a long snout. When the lamb is discovered, Mak's Wife promptly pretends that it is a changeling just left by an elf. The Shepherds, after punishing Mak by tossing him in a blanket, return to their flock; and almost immediately the Angel above sings to them the glad tidings of Christmas morn. Here is a comic action, complete in itself and quite detachable from the mystery, with which, indeed, it has no necessary connection. Perhaps it is even older than the mystery, and was inserted into the text merely to supply what is known nowadays as "comic relief,"—just as the farce of the 'Tub' might have been incorporated into a passion-play without any protest from the public.

Both in French and in English the comic scenes of the mysteries were often wholly irrelevant in theme and absolutely incongruous in treatment. No reverence for the sacred subject prevented the medieval audience from enjoying a joke, or made it very particular as to the quality of the fun it laughed at. Just as we moderns are surprised by the grinning gargoyles and by the satiric carvings of the mighty cathedrals, so in the medieval drama we are often taken aback by the bold vulgarity of the comic scenes. Altho the medieval writers had not found out that brevity is the soul of wit, they often acted on the belief that breadth is the body of humor. The authors were plain of speech and the audiences were never squeamish; and as we study what was then to be seen on the stage we are reminded of Taine's remark that in the middle ages man lived on a dunghill. It must be noted that the farces are rather more reprehensible than the comic scenes of the mysteries; and yet the grossest of these farces might be performed sometimes as the prelude to a miracle-play; thus the ' Miller ' preceded a very devout dramatization of the legend of Saint Martin. This low humor is indecorous rather than demoralizing; it shocks our sense of propriety sometimes, but it is never insidious or seductive. It was intended for the entertainment of the populace, which is often vulgar but which is rarely vicious. In the farces, as in the more serious scenes of the passion-plays, we can always see the simplicity and the sincerity which were ever the two chief characteristics of medieval endeavor.

IV

THE change from the Latin language to the speech of the people, the transfer of control from the clergy to the laity, the removal from the inside of the church to the outside, were all made gradually and tentatively, and with no intent to bring about any radical transformation. When the laymen took charge, they desired to do just what the priests had done, no more and no less; and if we seek to understand the circumstances of the performance outside of the church, we must recall what the conditions were originally inside the sacred edifice. In the cycle of the Nativity we saw that the manger was set up near the altar, and that not far distant there was erected a throne for Herod. Each of these places was thus what came to be known as a "station"; and the action of the play went on, not only at the one or the other of the stations, but also in other parts of the church, extending now and again even to the doors. The Easter cycle would also require several stations,—three at least, one with a throne for Pilate, another with the cross, a third with the open grave. The acting of the play was carried on chiefly in the open space between and in front of the several stations, the characters belonging to each of these remaining there, silent and motionless, until the time came for them to enter with the story. Then they might leave the station for a while, and go out into the open space, only to return to their own places so soon as the progress of the plot called for the characters of some other station.

When the Christmas cycle and the Easter cycle were combined together, and when the few intermediate scenes were also cast into dialog, so that the whole earthly life of Jesus might be shown, from his birth to his resurrection, then the nave of the church would be inconveniently crowded with the many stations requisite for the whole gospel-story; and there would be left between them, and in front, an inadequate area for what might be termed the neutral ground, the open space for the acting of the many scenes which did not call for special stations—such, for instance, as the Entry into Jerusalem, or the Betrayal at Gethsemane. Those who began to act out the sacred story in the church had no thought of scenery,—which, indeed, was a thing to them not only unknown, but wholly inconceivable. They were seeking to show what had happened on the very day they were commemorating. Even when the incidents had cohered into a sequence, it was the action itself that was all-important, and the place where it came to pass was without significance except when it needed to be specified. So the most of the acting was always in the more open space in the center; and stations were utilized only when they were really necessary. Probably as the mysteries increased in length the number of necessary stations became cumbersome, and only in the larger cathedrals would it be possible to avoid an awkward cluttering within the chancel. Quite possibly, this multiplication was an added reason for removing the performance of the mysteries outside the church, to some ampler place, where the several stations might be more widely separated.

When this removal did take place, and the mysteries were presented in the open air, what the laymen who took charge of them would undoubtedly seek to do would be to preserve carefully such traditions as had been established in the course of the performances given by the clergy. These laymen would therefore avail themselves of the device of the stations, modifying these as might be required by the new conditions of the performance. In England this modification came in time to be somewhat different from that obtaining in France; but as the English mystery is derived from French models, the French form demands attention first, the more so as elsewhere in Europe there is a closer resemblance to French usage than to English.

In France, then, a mystery would be acted upon a platform put up in some public place, often in the open square in front of the cathedral. To provide reserved seats for the dignitaries of the church, the officials of the city, and the distinguished strangers invited to attend, grand stands would be erected facing the platform and along the sides, the central area being left free for the populace, who were always eager to crowd in, while the gaily draped windows of the surrounding houses would be available as private boxes. The platform, intended to serve as a stage, was perhaps a hundred and fifty feet long, and some fifty or sixty feet deep. The front part was generally free and clear, so that the actors could move to and fro, while at the back were ranged the stations—which in France came soon to be known as "mansions." At the extreme left of the spectators, and raised high on pillars, was Heaven, wherein God sat, often with a gilded face, the better to suggest the shining glory of his countenance. At the extreme right of the spectators was Hell-mouth, the fiery cavern where the Devil and all his imps had their abode. Then stretching from Heaven to Hell-mouth was the line of mansions, those earliest in use being on the left. A wall, pierced by a door, might indicate Nazareth; next an altar covered by a canopy and protected by a balustrade would suggest the Temple; and a second wall with its gate could serve to call up the idea of Jerusalem itself. In

the center there might be a more elaborate construction, with columns and a throne, intended
for the palace of Pontius Pilate. A third wall with
two doors might be made to serve as the house
of the high-priest and as the Golden Gate; while
in front of this and not far from Hell-mouth there
might be a tank of real water, with a little boat float-
ing on it, so as to simulate the Sea of Gennesaret.

These are the mansions that are depicted in a
miniature on the manuscript of a mystery acted
in Valenciennes in the middle of the sixteenth
century. In other places, and at other times,
there might be more or there might be less, for
there was never any uniformity of custom; and
even here we see that many of the most important episodes of the gospel-narrative must have
been performed on the front part of the platform
and wholly unrelated to any of the mansions
ranged at the back. The mansions were employed
only when certain portions of the sacred story
could, by their use, be made clearer or more
striking; and even when they were set up, however elaborate their decoration might be, it was
never in any way deceptive. The mansions were
not intended actually to represent the special
places; the most they were expected to do was to
suggest them so that a few columns would indicate a palace or a temple, and so that a wall and a
door sufficed to evoke the idea of a city.

Thus we see that in France the stations used inside the church were set up side by side on the open-air stage outside of the church, where they were known as mansions. In England, when the passion-play was taken out of the sacred edifice, another arrangement was adopted: the stations were separated and each was shown by itself, being called a "pageant." Sometimes these were immovable, and sometimes they were ambulatory; and in the latter case, which seems to have been the more frequent, the pageant was apparently not unlike the elaborately decorated "floats" familiar in modern parades, such as that of Mardi Gras in New Orleans. Corpus Christi day was early chosen as the festival most fit for the performance of the mysteries; and in Great Britain the pageants followed in the wake of the Corpus Christi procession through the town. The first pageant, with its appropriate decorations and its own group of performers, would draw up before the church-door as the end of the procession emerged therefrom; and the first episode of the play would then be represented there, sometimes on the broad platform of the wagon, but often in the street itself,—just as most of the acting in the French mysteries took place not so much in the mansions themselves as in the neutral ground in the front of the stage. One stage-direction in an English manuscript is curiously

135

for each of the important episodes of the play, thus recalling the original stations devised for the performance when it took place inside of the church. The spectators, following the procession, would halt in front of the first platform and witness the acting of the first episode; and when that was concluded they would pass along to the second platform to behold the second episode; and so on until they had seen the entire mystery. The English were thus setting up separately the stations which the French had preferred to put side by side upon one very long platform. But these variations of custom between the French and the English are external only, and of no immediate importance, altho they account in part for the divergence to be observed in the development of the later dramatic literatures of the two languages.

Essentially the mystery is the same, wherever it is acted, and in whatever language, French or English, German or Italian. It is the same in its long-windedness and in its loose-jointedness, in its homely directness of speech alternating with turgid bombast, in its occasional touches of genuine feeling and of unstrained pathos, in the introduction of humorous scenes, in the frank realism of dialog, and, above all, in the simple faith of those who wrote it, of those who acted it, and of those who beheld its performance. The influence of the audience must always be taken into account: and the medieval spectators for whose edification the mystery was devised were unlearned and without culture; they were ignorant and even gross; they had no tincture of letters; they were credulous and superstitious and wonder-loving; they were at once devout and irreverent,—or at least they seem so to us; they had a liking for broad fun and for a robust realism of treatment; they were shocked by no vulgarity and they resented no incongruity, for they were wholly devoid of the historic sense (as we moderns call it).

Altho the English mysteries were of Anglo-Norman origin and follow the French tradition in the main, yet the bond of unity was broken when Latin was abandoned for the vernacular; and there are other differences between the performances in French and those in English besides the modification of the station into the mansion in the one country and into the pageant in the other. In England, the entire mystery—shortened now and again by the occasional omission of one episode or another—seems sometimes to have been presented in a single day, the exhibition beginning as early as four in the morning. In France the performance was more likely to continue over several successive days, very much as the Wagnerian cycle is now given at Bayreuth,—altho it may be doubted whether any modern audience

could have the patience of the medieval spectators of Bourges who in the sixteenth century
were entertained by a mystery of the 'Acts of
the Apostles,' the performance of which took
forty days.

In England, as we have seen, the pageants followed the religious procession; whereas in France,
where the mansions were immovable on a single
platform, it was not unusual for the whole troop
of performers to make a street-parade before the
acting began, quite in the manner of the modern
traveling circus. In France, again, when the
church gave up the control of the mysteries, they
were turned over to lay organizations of burghers,
founded especially to perform the sacred plays;
whereas in England this task was assumed by
the gilds, each of which undertook the episode
which its craftsmanship best fitted it to carry out,
the Carpenters, for instance, being responsible
for Noah's Ark, and the Goldsmiths undertaking
the Three Kings, because they could best provide
the royal diadems.

Further differences there are also between the
mysteries as performed in France or in England
and the sacred-representations of the Italians;
and again between the dramatizations of the
Scriptures as acted in Germany and those to be
seen in Spain. But these differences are matters
of detail merely; and the line of development was

everywhere the same throughout those parts of
Europe that had been ruled by Rome. Everywhere also was the production of a mystery
considered as a good deed, as an act pleasing to
Heaven, and certain to win favor from the Deity
and from the saints. Such performances were
often, therefore, given in a season of pesti-
lence to placate the wrath of God or to deserve
the protection of some particular saint. Such an
exhibition took place in Constantinople, within
Saint Sophia itself, in the middle of the fifteenth
century, just before the capture of the capital
of the Western Empire by the Turks. Mysteries were also performed in certain towns after
an escape from impending danger and as a testimony of gratitude to Heaven for its intervention;
and it is to this sentiment that we owe the continued performance of the passion-play, which is
still to be seen every tenth summer at Oberam-
mergau.

The majority of the mysteries preserved to us
in manuscript are anonymous, and of only a
few are we acquainted with the exact date
of composition. Most of the authors are to be
considered rather as compilers; lacking individuality, they were satisfied to accept the play
as they found it, modifying the framework but
little after it had once been constructed, and
satisfying themselves with adding or subtracting

episodes at will. Each of them freely availed himself of the labors of those of his predecessors with which he chanced to be familiar. Sometimes he rewrote what he borrowed, and sometimes he copied it slavishly, careless of any diversity of diction. So there is not often harmony of style in any single mystery; and yet there is an immense monotony when a number of them are compared together.

V

VERY closely allied to the mystery was the miracle-play, which may have come into being even before the Easter cycle had elaborated itself into a passion-play. A sequence of episodes taken from Holy Writ we now call a mystery; and what we now call a miracle-play is a sequence of episodes taken from the life of some wonder-working saint. In England the mystery was much the more frequent; but in France the miracle-play was perhaps the more popular, as it was probably almost as ancient. Indeed, in the middle ages no one seems ever to have made any distinction between the two kinds of play, as the medieval mind was not trained to discriminate between the canonical books and the Apocrypha, or even between the Scriptures and the legends of the saints. In miracle-play, as in mystery, we find the same naïf treatment of life, the same panoramic construction of the story, the same admixture of comic incidents, and the same apparent irreverence; and the circumstances of the performance would be the same also.

The middle ages had an appetite for allegory quite as vigorous as the liking for legend; and after the saintly biographies had been set on the stage as miracle-plays, allegory was also cast into dialog, and thus we have the moral-plays. The morality was a medieval forerunner of our modern novel-with-a-purpose, as unconvincingly didactic as it is inevitably dull. The morality may even be defined as an attempt to dramatize a sermon,—whereas the mystery is simply a dramatization of the text. Written to be presented before an audience used to the primitive methods of the passion-play, the authors make free use of the device of the stations, for instance. In one morality, the ' Castle of Constancy,' there were six stations: one was a castellated structure open below to reveal a bed for the chief character, who personified the Human Race; and the other five stations were disposed around this loftier stage, one in the east for God, one in the northeast for Greed, one in the west for the World, one in the south for the Flesh, and one in the north for the Devil. The hero of this string of argumentative conversations, Human Race, appears at first as a child, and the Angels of Good and of Evil come to him. He is tempted off to the World by the Evil Angel; and later, as a young man, he is introduced to the Seven Deadly Sins. In time Repentance leads him to Confession; and as a man of forty we see him in the Castle of Constancy, surrounded by the Seven Most Excellent Virtues. Thereupon the Castle itself is besieged by the three evil powers and the Seven Deadly Sins and their allies. Then at last, as an old man, Human Race backslides again, and the Evil Angel is bearing him away, when a formal trial takes place before God, at which Justice and Truth accuse him, while he is defended by Mercy and Peace.

The morality was an attempt to depict character, but with the aid of violent colors only, and with a harsh juxtaposition of light and darkness. Yet it helped along the development of the drama in that it permitted a freer handling of the action, since the writer of moralities had always to invent his plots, whereas the maker of mysteries had his stories ready-made to his hand. The morality was frankly fiction, while the miracle-play gave itself out for fact. Then, also, the tendency seems irresistible for an author who has any appreciation of human nature to go speedily from the abstract to the concrete and to substitute for the cold figure of Pride itself the less frigid portrait of an actual man who is proud. Thus mere allegory, barren and chill, is swiftly warmed into social satire, tingling with individuality; and so we have here before us the germ out of which a living comedy was to be evolved. It is to be noted that when the morality had achieved a certain freedom for itself in plot and in character, it seems to have exerted a healthy influence upon the contemporary mystery and miracle-play.

In fact, the medieval mind did not distinguish the three kinds of drama sharply, and we find them commingled in more than one example,— notably in the English ' Mary Magdalene.' We discover the same confusion of species in all uncritical periods, when production is spontaneous and unconscious. In method the mystery and the miracle-play are alike; and by no certain mark can we set off the morality from the interlude in English or the monolog from the burlesque-sermon in French. The more elevated the effort, the more likely was an admixture of the grotesque. Immediately before or after the loftiest moments of a tragic theme, the nimble devils would come capering forth to make the spectator shriek with laughter at their buffoonery as they bore away some evil-doer to be cast into Hell-mouth.

Popular as these plays were, it is only in a chance episode that any one of them is really raised into literature. The drama must be the most democratic of all the arts, since its very exis-

tence depends on the multitude; and it is therefore
likely always to represent the average intelligence
of any era. The long period known as the middle ages, whatever its literary unattractiveness,
brought about a new birth of the acted drama.
It aroused in the people the desire for the pleasures of the theater; and it began to train actors
against the time when acting should once more
become a profession.

In considering the deficiencies of the medieval
drama, we must never forget that the actors
were all amateurs,—priests at first, and then
burghers and craftsmen, students and clerks.
They might be paid for their services, or they
might choose to perform as a labor of love; but
acting was not their calling, and their opportu-
nities for improving themselves in the art were
infrequent. The accomplished actor stimulates
the dramatist, and the playwright is ever developing the performer; each is necessary to the
other, and in the middle ages we find neither.
Yet slowly the traditions of a theater were getting themselves established. There was acting,
such as it was; there were plays, such as they
were, not so much dramas as mere panoramas of
successive episodes; there were audiences, rude
and gross, no doubt, but composed of human
beings, after all, and therefore ever ready to be
entranced and thrilled by the art of the master-

craftsman. But in the medieval drama we seek in vain for a master-craftsman; he is not to be found in France or in England, in Spain, in Italy, or in Germany. The elements of a vital drama were all there, ready to the hand of a true dramatist who might know how to make use of them; they were awaiting the grasp of a poet-playwright who might be able to present with technical skill and with imaginative insight the perpetual struggle of good and evil, of God and the Devil.

But in all medieval literature there is no born playwright; and there is no born poet who wrought in dialog and action. The one indestructible work of art which gives utterance to the intentions of the middle ages, to the ideals of that dark time, and to its aspirations, was not made to be represented within the church or out of it, either by priests or by laymen, even tho it bore the name of the 'Divine Comedy.'

V. THE DRAMA IN SPAIN

I

IN the middle ages a simple sort of drama had
been slowly evolved out of the liturgy of the
church; it had grown sturdily until in time it
was strong enough to stand on its own feet; it
took over the primitive farce of the strolling jesters
and thus supplied itself with the comic contrast
needful in any adequate representation of life; it
spoke the language of the people and it embodied
their beliefs and their aspirations; in short, altho
it was as yet clumsily inartistic and frankly unliterary, it was at least alive; and it had won its
right to survive.   A single brief scene acted in
the church, by the priests themselves, and in
Latin, had slowly led to the performance of a
sequence of scenes, in the vernacular, by laymen,
outside of the church.   The mystery, which was
a sequence of scenes in the life of Jesus, had a rival
in the miracle-play, which was a sequence of scenes
in the life of some wonder-working saint.   Dis-
regarding the invisible line that divided the sacred

from the profane, the medieval drama was in time able to take as the central figure of its straggling episodes a hero of secular legend or of romantic narrative, or even of actual fact. So the chronicle-play came into being, and the "history," such as we see it in Shakspere; and while the miracle-play was intended to be exhibited gratuitously, in an open square, by bands of amateurs, upon some special occasion, the later chronicle-play was prepared to be performed by professional actors, at regular intervals, in a building set apart for the purpose, before an audience that had paid its way in.

It was at this moment of the development of the medieval drama that the Renascence arrived, bringing with it the masterpieces of ancient art. Scholars in love with the severe beauty of Greek tragedy turned with disgust from the formlessness and the vulgarity of the popular performances. They could not know then that the Attic stage had grown out of beginnings quite as humble, and that the medieval drama needed only to be lifted into literature, just as the crude Hellenic dialog and chorus had been elevated by the power of the poet who had accepted the primitive form, filling it with the might of his genius. They did not perceive that the massive simplicity of Sophocles was due partly to the conditions under which his tragedies had been performed in the

Theater of Dionysus,—conditions wholly unlike those obtaining in western Europe two thousand years later. Indeed, the scholars of the Renascence gave little thought to the actual performance, devoting their attention chiefly to the merely literary merits of the ancient dramatic poets, and accepting as the model to be followed not so much Sophocles, the marvelous playwright, as the unactable Seneca. They were impatient to thrust on one side the rude but living drama of their own day, in order to make room for imitations,—and imitations rather of the clever Hispano-Roman rhetorician than of the noble Athenian dramatist. They did not perceive the vigorous vitality of the chronicle-play, which had established itself solidly in conformity with the actual conditions of the medieval theater; and they could not suspect that the plain people were right in clinging to the existing drama, shapeless as it was, and in resisting all attempts to substitute for it a merely literary exercise.

The chronicle-play was artless enough, but it was exactly suited to its public; it had a stage of its own, and actors to perform it, and audiences to enjoy it; and all that it needed was that the poets should perceive its possibilities, and that they should accept it as it was, biding their time to cleanse it from its vulgarities, to bestow on it the art it lacked, and to give it the harmony and

149

proportion it had neglected. The example of the great dramatists of antiquity could not but be useful to the poets who might attempt this purification of the drama of the middle ages; and the study not only of Sophocles, but even of Seneca, might be serviceable. And, as a matter of fact, we find that in the several modern languages a dramatic literature has come into existence only when successive poets have taken the popular form as they found it, and tried to give it something of the unity, the propriety, and the dignity which they had admired in the classics of Greece and Rome.

This is what happened in Spanish, in English, and in French; and in these languages the modern drama is an outgrowth of the medieval, modified more or less by the acceptance of the classic models. This influence of the ancients is most obvious in the French theater and least evident in the Spanish, while in the English it is pervasive rather than paraded. In Italy the scholars were opinionated and intolerant; the poets scorned the medieval drama, both serious and humorous, sacred-representations and comedy-of-masks; they insisted on casting aside all that the middle ages had accomplished and on returning absolutely to antiquity. The Italian men-of-letters did not firmly grasp the fact that a living drama is always the result of a long partnership between the audiences and the actors, and that it is always conditioned by the circumstances of its performance, including the traditions of the actual theater. As a result of this hostile attitude on the part of the leaders of the new culture, we discover that the Italians developed no dramatic literature of their own. We perceive that their efforts resulted in little more than a few lifeless imitations from the antique, acted by main strength now and again, but failing absolutely to establish a new tradition in the theater itself. We observe also that the main body of the Italian public had to satisfy its desire for the drama with the unliterary and semi-acrobatic comedy-of-masks.

Perhaps it was this dearth of a living dramatic literature in their own language which helped to lead the Italian critics astray in their ingenious deduction of a code for the control of dramatic poetry. They spurned the only plays they had had occasion to see actually performed; and with the intellectual subtlety of their race at that epoch, they got together a body of rules, not exactly evolved out of their inner consciousness, but derived from their misinterpretation of what Horace and Aristotle had said. Misguided by what they had misread in the Roman lyrist (who had also no acted drama to sustain his theories) and by what they read into the Greek philosopher (who was specifically analyzing the Attic drama only, that being the sole theater he could know anything about), the Italian critics proceeded to set up the standard of the Three Unities,— the Unity of Action, the Unity of Time, and the Unity of Place, — insisting that a tragedy should have a single story to be completed in a single day and to be shown in a single place.

They persuaded not only themselves, but also the men-of-letters of all the other countries where the new learning established itself, that an acceptance of these rigid limitations was obligatory upon all the dramatic poets who might seek to follow in the footsteps of the ancients. But fortunately they were never able to convince the unlearned public that it was wise to insist on these arbitrary restrictions; and so it was that the practical playwrights, who were trying to interest the plain people, did not find themselves forced to enter the triple-barred cage of the Unities. The critics might protest shrilly, but the dramatists kept on working in freedom; and when the spectator had been amused by a play he never cared to raise any objection, even if the action did ramble along for many days and in many places.

We can see now that the Athenian audiences were in reality not more exacting than the English or the Spanish, since the code the Italian critics promulgated had often been violated in anticipation by the Attic dramatists. Even the

Unity of Action is not always discoverable in a Greek play; and it is due to the accidental conditions of the performance in the Theater of Dionysus that the Unity of Time and the Unity of Place may seem generally to be observed. But altho the common sense of the broad public refused to hamper the playwright by needless limitations of his liberty, the plays of the Greeks were not without immediate and abiding influence upon modern dramatic literature. In the course of the years, the severe restraint of the Attic drama and its majestic movement made a profound impression upon the popular playwrights, who began to choose loftier themes and to build their plots more artfully. Slowly the string of episodes came to be knit more closely together and the central characters came to be more veraciously brought out. The struggle, which is at the core of every good play, was more clearly seized and more boldly presented.

In all the modern languages, the loftier drama is the result of a stimulation of the actual folkplay, as we find it in the middle ages, by the study of a model supplied by the Attic stage directly or indirectly. The modern drama is due to a fecundation of the medieval by the antique. Of the new dramatic literatures thus elaborated from unliterary beginnings, one may owe more than another to the example of the great Greeks;

but all of them owe much,— even the Spanish,
in which the influence of the Renascence is least
obvious.

II

THE Renascence has been called the bridge which
connects the middle ages with modern life,— a
bridge more than one span of which was built
out of the relics of antiquity; and altho it would
be an overstatement to assert that the most of
the Spanish people did not care to go over to the
new world of thought explored by the leaders of
the Renascence, it is not too much to suggest that
those of the Spaniards who did venture across
carried over with them more medieval characteristics than the Italians or the French burdened
themselves with. The Renascence was, above all
things else, an emancipation of the human intelligence; it was a declaration of independence put
at once into deeds; and this gift of freedom the
Spanish people had no wish to accept. In fact,
they were glad to reject it, for among them there
was no parallel to the questioning curiosity of
the Italians, to the speculative liberty of the Germans, and to the mental alertness of the English.
Willingly they had accepted the guidance of the
Inquisition; and to them the liberation of man's
spirit was not only unwelcome,— it was even
abhorrent. The Spaniards had no sympathy

with the sensuous joyousness, the sheer delight in living, which stands out as an essential element of the Renascence. The Spanish ideals were ever ascetic and mystic,—whatever might be their actual practices. However much they might in fact enjoy life, in theory at least they held it to be only a dark valley of transition; and here the Madrid of Philip is as opposite as possible to the London of Elizabeth and the Florence of the Medici, as well as to the Athens of Pericles.

The evidence of this hostile attitude toward the newer ways of thinking is abundant on every page of Spanish history and in every contribution to Spanish literature; and nowhere is it more clearly visible than in the Spanish drama, which even in its best days is far more closely related to the medieval drama than is the later drama of France or even of England. In the splendid epoch of Lope de Vega and of Calderon and of the throng of inventive playwrights that encompasses them about, the Spanish drama is strangely similar to the drama of the middle ages. It is loose in its construction, careless of proportion, never afraid of monotony of topic, full of repetitions, devoid of concentration. It has always an air of improvisation; and altho it is never quite so unliterary as were most of the mysteries and the miracle-plays, it rarely attains conciseness of speech or polish of phrase; and very seldom indeed does it aspire to a true harmony of plot. It is as reckless in anachronism, and it reveals the same absence of the historic sense which is so distinct a characteristic of the medieval writers, to whom, as it has been well said, "past centuries seemed to form only a single and grand epoch in which were united all the celebrities of history." It deals with actions chiefly, but occasionally with emotions, and almost never with thought. Its temper is uncritical; and its tone is sometimes even more superstitious than was common in the medieval plays. Of course, the Spanish playwrights soon attained a technical skill such as no one of the unknown scribes of the middle ages could achieve; and indeed it is this dramaturgic adroitness which saliently differentiates the brisk Spanish plays from their lumbering medieval predecessors.

The rise of the theater in Spain was aided by two circumstances which were lacking in Italy. The Spanish had achieved their unity as the result of a strenuous effort sustained for years,— an effort which had stiffened the national will and aroused the national consciousness; and they had found at last a focus of national life in their new capital, where the dramatist could make sure of all sorts of spectators. The Spaniards also shared with the English a gift not bestowed on the Italians,— they were makers of ballads; and they had thus supplied themselves with an abundance of the material most fit for the playwright to handle, while the making of the ballads had helped to train their poets to deal directly and simply with situation and with character.

Throughout western Europe the folk-theater of the middle ages is very much the same everywhere; and in France as in England, in Italy as in Spain, we are shocked by the same irreverent commingling of the sacred and the profane, and by the same obtrusion of realistic farce into plays intended for edification. For a while this gross incongruity was accepted with only slight protest; but after heroes from history and from romance had been substituted for the saints, and after the humor of the comic episodes had been broadened beyond the borders of decency, the ecclesiastical authorities sometimes became aware of the objectionable features. In Spain, for example, a formal law forbade a priest from taking part in "scornful plays" or from attending them; and it declared that such plays should not be performed in the churches. But the same law specifically authorized a priest to act in representations of the Nativity and of the Resurrection. "Such things as these move men to do well and be devout in the faith, and may be done in order to remind them that they really happened. But they must be performed with great decency and devotion in the large cities, where there are arch-bishops and bishops who may order them, and they must not be represented in villages nor poor places, or for the purpose of gain."

If this law was actually enforced, the villages and poor places could have had no other theatrical entertainment than that supplied by little bands of strolling players. These were probably as prevalent in Spain as in Italy and in France; and their repertory was as primitive. The leader of one such company was Lope de Rueda, who is hailed as the founder of the Spanish theater, — very much as Thespis is held to be the beginner of the Greek drama. He was at once sole play-wright and chief performer. Cervantes tells us that "in the time of this celebrated Spaniard, all the apparatus of a manager was contained in a bag, and consisted of four white shepherd's jackets, bordered with gilt leather, four beards and wigs, and four shepherd's crooks, more or less. . . . The stage was merely composed of four square blocks of wood, upon which rested five or six boards, that were thus raised about four palms from the ground. . . . The furniture was an old blanket hung on two cords, making what they call the dressing-room, behind which were the musicians, who sang old ballads with-out a guitar." Here we find in Spain, just as we can find also in Greece a score of centuries earlier, one important actor accompanied by a few singers, performing upon a platform set up in the market-place with an improvised dressing-tent behind it.

Exactly what kind of play it was that Thespis was wont to act in his wanderings we can now only guess; but by good fortune certain of the simple pieces of Lope de Rueda have been preserved. They are very simple indeed; but they have the same open fidelity to the facts of life that we find in the English scene of Mak and the Shepherds and in the French farce of the 'Tub'; and they are sustained by the same humorous observation of human nature. One of them, entitled the 'Olives,' begins with the stepping up upon the stage of a Peasant, who calls his Wife. His Daughter it is who comes out from behind the dressing-room curtain, to say that her mother is at a neighbor's. While the Peasant scolds, the Wife returns, and bids her Daughter cook the father's supper. Then she asks if the Peasant has done as he promised,— if he has planted the olive-tree? When she learns that this has been attended to, she foresees that in six or seven years the tree will yield them several measures of olives and that by planting the branches from time to time they will have a field of olives in a score of years; and then the Daughter will sell them for two reals a peck. At this the Peasant protests; the olives are not worth such a price.

The Wife declares that they are, the tree being from Cordova; and in spite of her husband's objections, she turns to the Daughter and orders the girl to charge two reals. The Peasant calls the Daughter and bids her obey her father and not ask so much. The Wife insists on the girl's selling the olives for two reals. The Peasant furiously threatens to beat the child if she does not do as he tells her; and thereupon the Wife, also moved to anger, begins actually to beat the girl for disobedience. While the Daughter is beseeching both father and mother not to kill her, a Neighbor steps up on the stage to ask the reason of the outcry. The Peasant explains that the cause of dispute is the price to be asked for certain olives, and the Neighbor naturally asks to see them that he may judge for himself. When he is told that the tree is only that day planted and that the fruit they are quarreling about will not be gathered for many years, he laughs at them all, crying, "What an absurd quarrel! Who ever saw the like? The olives are scarcely planted — and yet they cause the poor girl to cry."

Nothing could be more unpretending than this little scene; and its most valuable quality was that it was perfectly portable, and that it called for neither scenery nor costumes. It could be acted wherever and whenever four performers happened to be banded together. Quite as elementary as the 'Olives' is the 'Blind Beggars and the Boy,' written by a friend and follower of Lope de Rueda's, Juan de Timoneda.   One Blind Beggar enters and whines forth his customary chant of entreaty.   The other Blind Beggar comes on from the opposite side and also intones his prayer for alms.   A Boy crosses the stage, and as he sees the first Blind Beggar he is about to flee, recognizing the master he has robbed and deserted.   Then the urchin remembers that, since his master cannot see him, he is safe so long as he keeps quiet.   After a time, the two Blind Beggars drop into chat with each other, while the Boy listens.   Believing themselves to be alone, the two Blind Beggars discuss the advantages and disadvantages of their calling; and at last the first tells the second how he has been robbed by his rascally boy.   The second then explains how he protects himself by always carrying his ducats sewed in his cap,—whereupon the Boy steals forward, knocks off the precious cap, and escapes with it.   The owner naturally supposes that it is the man he has been speaking with who has taken the cap, and he asks for its return; but of course the other at once denies all knowledge of it.   Here is matter for a swift quarrel; and the little play ends with the two Blind Beggars engaged in an angry fight.

Even before the populace had been easily

amused by lively trifles like these, and while the mystery was still at the hight of its vogue, professed poets had sought to imitate the more scholarly attempts of the Italian men-of-letters. They had devised pastoral-plays, of varying poetic merit but always of a hopeless artificiality. If any of these pastoral-plays happened to be actually performed, it was always by amateurs, for they were written to delight a noble or a royal patron, much as masques were in England not long after and the later mythological ballets of the French court. They were none of them composed to please a real public that had paid its money to see a genuine play; and, as might be expected, they seem to have had little or no influence on the growth of the acted drama. Until Lope de Rueda was followed by Lope de Vega, the literary play was not popular and the popular play was not literary. It was Lope de Vega who accepted the popular drama, such as it was, and gave it the art it lacked.

It is to be noted that one great figure intervenes between Lope de Rueda and Lope de Vega— the figure of Cervantes, the greatest in all Spanish literature. A score or more plays did Cervantes write; and they were actually acted with some small measure of success or — to use the words of the author himself—"without their receiving tribute of cucumbers or other missiles." Of those early attempts two survive to show that Cervantes, like Balzac and like Tolstoi, had only a moderate share of play-making ability. They are not without merit, of course, for they came from the pen of Cervantes; but they are cumbrous, and sluggish, and almost as ill proportioned as the mysteries upon which they are modeled; they are wholly without the briskness and the pleasant inventiveness which Lope de Vega was soon to bestow on the Spanish drama. That Cervantes was lacking in the dramaturgic faculty is made evident again by the plays which he published later in life, after Lope had set up a new standard. Indisputable is it that Cervantes was far more richly endowed than Lope, and also that his single splendid achievement in fiction outweighs all that Lope ever accomplished in all the departments of literature; but equally undeniable is it that Lope had the one thing needful for success upon the stage, and that this was precisely the qualification which Cervantes wanted.

III

Lope molded the Spanish drama to suit his own gifts; he stamped it forever with the impress of his own personality; and even if we must admit that Calderon, who came after, also rose higher, and that the younger poet surpassed the elder in the lyrical elevation of several of his plays, none the less must we remember always that the greatest dramas of Calderon are examples of a class of which Lope had set the first model. If we acknowledge, as we may, that even Calderon trod only where Lope had first broken the path, we must record that all the other dramatists of Spain were also followers in his footsteps. From out the numerous mass of Lope de Vega's works, it would be possible to select a satisfactory specimen of every species of the drama as it has existed in Spain. What Lope was, so was the Spanish drama. He came first, and he was the most original of all, the most fertile, the most indefatigable, the most various, the most multifarious.

His influence on the stage of Spain was far more potent and more durable than that of Sophocles on the theater of Greece or of Shakspere on the drama of England. It was Lope who earliest discovered how to hold the interest of a modern audience by the easy intricacy of his story and by the surprising variety of the successive situations, each artfully prepared for by its predecessor. If Schlegel found an ingenious felicity of plot-making to be so characteristic of the Spanish drama that he was led to suspect a Spanish origin for any play in which he observed this quality, it was to the practice and to the precept of Lope de Vega that his fellow-dramatists owed their possession of this merit. One of these fellow-dramatists it was who summed up the good points of the Spanish drama in lines which have been thus Englished by G. H. Lewes:

> Invention, interest, sprightly turns in plays,
> Say what they will, are Spain's peculiar praise ;
> Hers are the plots which strict attention seize,
> Full of intrigue and yet disclosed with ease :
> Hence scenes and acts her fertile stage affords
> Unknown, unrivaled on the foreign boards.

It was the lack of a metropolis which had helped to deprive the Italians of a drama worthy of their intellectual supremacy in the early Renascence; and it was the choice of Madrid as the capital which made possible the sudden outflowering of the Spanish dramatic literature. The many little bands of strolling players, similar to the company Lope de Rueda had directed, and containing performers of both sexes, looked longingly toward the court; and two of them were in time allowed to settle in the royal city, bringing with them their elementary repertory of songs and dances, of simple interludes and of lumbering chronicle-plays. The theater assigned to each of these companies was as primitive as the entertainment they proffered, for it was no more than the court-yard of a house. At the farther end of this court-yard was the shallow platform, which served as a stage, and which was shielded by a sloping roof. Near to the stage were a few benches, and then came the space where the main body of the rude public stood throughout the performance, unprotected from the weather. Behind them rose several tiers of seats, stretching back almost to the house, and affording accommodation for the women, who were kept apart from the men. Then the rooms of the house itself served as private boxes; and in time these came to be so highly valued that the right to one passed as an heirloom. A few privileged spectators were allowed seats on the sides of the stage. There was neither curtain nor scenery.

The performance took place by daylight in the early afternoon, so there was no need of artificial illumination. It began with the appearance of the musicians upon the stage itself, where they played on the guitar and sang popular ballads until an acceptable audience had gathered or until the boisterous impatience of those who had arrived compelled the actors to commence. Then the musicians withdrew; and a chief performer, often the manager himself, appeared to speak a prolog, amusing in itself and abounding in compliments to the audience. When at last he left the stage free, the actors who were to open the play came out and the first act was performed. Simple as was the medieval stage with its neutral ground backed by the stations, which became mansions in France and pageants in England, the Spanish stage was simpler still, since the stations were abolished and there remained only the neutral ground — the bare platform. Neither authors nor spectators ever bothered themselves about the place where the characters were at any moment supposed to be. The actors then engaged in carrying on the story were standing in sight of the audience; and this was the sole essential, the background being merely accidental. If by chance it became necessary for the audience to know just where the action was about to take place, then this information was furnished by the dialog itself, without any change of the stage-setting, the platform remaining bare of all scenery. Thus the dramatist was at liberty to select such incidents of his fable as he saw fit, not having to consider the difficulty of making the successive places visible in the eyes of the spectators.

When the first act was ended the actors left the stage; the musicians came forward again; and there followed a song and dance or even a little ballad-farce to fill the interval between the acts of the chief play. Then the second act was presented in its turn; and after it there came another song and dance or another comical interlude. The third act of the play was always the last, for the Spanish dramatists early accepted a division into three parts. When the chief play was finally concluded, it was at once followed by a farce, and often also by one of the national dances; and then at last the entertainment came to an end, and the noisy and turbulent spectators withdrew, having applauded boisterously if they thought they had had their money's worth, and having with equal freedom made vocal their dissatisfaction if they did not happen to think so.

These were the apparently unfavorable conditions under which were represented the works of the dramatic poets of Spain at the moment when the drama flourished most exuberantly; and no one who knows the circumstances of the contemporary theater in England under Elizabeth can fail to perceive the striking similarity. The dramatic poets of England, like the dramatic poets of Spain, saw their plays produced by daylight, on an unadorned platform, set up in what was no more than the courtyard of an inn, open to the sky. The English plays, like the Spanish, were acted without scenery, before a noisy throng of groundlings who stood in the pit; and in England also there were what were called "jigs" by the clown between the acts. The English plays, like the Spanish, were devised to please the public as a whole and not to delight only a special class. Such differences as there are between the Spanish

drama and the English are due not to the conditions of the performance, but directly to the characteristics of the two peoples; and Shakspere is
not more representative of the Elizabethan Englishman than is Calderon of the contemporary
Spaniard.

In Spain, as in England, the people had given
proof that they possessed the first requisite of a
truly national drama, —a steadfast determination,
steeled for instant action.   The Spanish kingdom
was then seemingly at the very climax of its
might; and having compacted the monarchy and
driven out the Moors, having overrun half Europe
and taken all America as their own, the Spaniards had the pride of a chosen people.   They
thrilled with a consciousness of a lofty destiny,
while at the same time they accepted with enthusiasm feudal and chivalrous ideals of fidelity and
loyalty and honor.   Men of very varied individuality, they were united in their devotion to the
church, in which they had an unquestioning
faith, and to the King, who ruled by divine right
and who could do no wrong.   Lope de Vega,
for example, had been in his youth a soldier on
the Invincible Armada; and later he became a
familiar of the Holy Inquisition.   It is true that
the religious fervor of the Spaniards was often
only empty superstition; and that it was in no
wise incompatible with a strangely contorted

ethical code which approved of vengeance as a duty and justified murder to remove a stain from honor.

The Spanish language is a rich and sonorous tongue, as characteristic of the race that speaks it as is English or French; and in the hands of the dramatic poets Spanish lends itself readily to the display of an eloquence which only too often sinks into facile grandiloquence. One of the most marked peculiarities of these plays is a rhetorical redundancy which often rises into a lyrical copiousness, but which not infrequently also condenses itself into a sententious apothegm. The personages taking part are as likely to reveal a vehement luxuriance of phrase as they are to disclose a perverse subtlety of intellect. Formal and pompous their speech is on occasion; and at other times it is easy and natural, refreshing in its humorous lightness, sparkling with unpremeditated wit, and bristling with pungent proverbs. As we read these plays we are constantly reminded that Seneca and Lucan and Marcus Aurelius were all of them Spaniards.

IV

THESE characteristics of the language itself, and of the people that spoke the language, are familiar to all who know 'Don Quixote'; and they are

made visible in the plays of every Spanish dramatist, especially in those of Lope de Vega, because
there is scarcely any kind of drama which he
was not the first to attempt. He has left us
farces as slight in texture as those of Lope de
Rueda; mysteries more artfully put together than
those of the medieval scribes; chronicle-plays not
unlike those of his immediate predecessors, but
with a hightened dramatic interest; dramatized
ballads and romances far more skilfully wrought
than any seen on the stage before he took it for
his own. He gave a lyric grace to the briefer
religious plays, which were called sacramental-
acts; and he himself invented the play of plot
and intrigue and mystery which is known as the
comedy-of-cloak-and-sword. He showed the
same fertility of ingenuity in devising comedies
of incident and of character. He solidly constructed somber tragedies of honor and revenge.
He seems to have written hundreds of plays of
every kind and description; and scores of them
are still preserved in print. They vary greatly in
merit; many of them are mere improvisations;
but very few of them fail to display his dexterity,
his perfect understanding of the theater, his mastery of stagecraft.

The art of the playwright is a finer art to-day,
no doubt; it is at once firmer and more delicate
than was possible in the Spain which was just

emerging from the middle ages; but the dramatists of every modern language are greatly indebted to the models set by Lope de Vega,—
and none the less because the most of these later
writers are unconscious of their obligation. Nowhere has modern dramaturgic craftsmanship
been carried to a higher pitch of perfection than
in France; and it must never be forgotten that
the 'Cid,' the first of French tragedies, and the
'Liar,' the first of French comedies, were both of
them borrowed by Corneille from Spanish plays
written by contemporary disciples of Lope de
Vega's.

From out the immense mass of Lope de Vega's
dramatic works it is not easy to make choice of
any single play as truly typical. The selection is
indeed difficult when we have before us pieces
of so many different classes, from the sacramental-acts and from mere dramatized anecdotes
to comedies sometimes perfervidly lyrical and
sometimes frankly prosaic, from chronicle-plays
loosely epic in their structure to true tragedies
with an ever-increasing tensity of emotion. But
one of his most famous plays is the 'Star of
Seville,' and perhaps this will serve as well as
any to suggest his method of handling a story on
the stage.

The first act begins with the King of Castile
and his evil counselor, Arias, coming upon the

stage with two of the Alcaldes of Seville, who compliment the monarch on his arrival. After they withdraw, the King asks eagerly about a beautiful girl he had remarked as he entered the city. Arias tells him that she is Estrella, known as the Star of Seville because of her loveliness, and that she is a sister of Bustos Tabera. The King confesses his sudden passion, and sends Arias to fetch Bustos to him, hoping through the brother to get at the sister. Then two Officers enter in turn, each asking the King for a vacant governorship; but he dismisses them without deciding. Arias returns with Bustos, a man of blunt honesty, who is surprised when the King proffers the governorship to him. He conceals his suspicions when the King flatters him, asks about his family, and finally promises to provide a proper husband for his sister. After the men have left the stage Estrella enters, so that the spectators are supposed now to be witnesses of a scene in her home. Accompanying her is Don Sancho, to whom she is betrothed and with whom she exchanges protestations of love. Bustos appears and tells his friend of the King's intention of finding a fit husband for his sister; whereupon Don Sancho reproaches him for not having informed the monarch that their marriage had been agreed upon. When they depart, the King and Arias enter, and the dialog makes it clear that they are now to be imagined as standing at the door of Estrella's dwelling. The King has come to visit the brother in hope of getting speech with the sister: but Bustos, when he appears, finds excuses for not asking the King to enter the house. So the monarch takes the brother off with him, leaving Arias behind to corrupt the sister. When the stage is again left empty, Estrella enters with her maid-servant; and therefore the audience perceives that they are within the house as before. Arias presents himself to tell Estrella of the King's passion for her; but her sole answer is to turn her back on him and walk out of the room. Thereupon Arias promptly bribes the servant to admit the King that night. After they depart, there is a scene at the palace; Arias comes in to report, and the delighted monarch bids him see that the servant is well rewarded. Then the King and his evil counselor leave the stage empty and bring to an end the first act,— an act of swift and spirited exposition, taking the spectator at once into the heart of the situation and exciting the interest of expectancy.

The second act opens with the admission of the King into Estrella's house, and with the unexpected return of Bustos, who confronts the intruder in the dark and demands his name. The King has to declare himself; but the sturdy fellow pretends not to believe this, asserting that the monarch, being the fountain of honor, would never have come there to bring dishonor. The King is thus forced to cross swords with the subject, but he escapes unhurt as soon as the servants bring lights. Bustos hangs the treacherous maid-servant, and bids his sister prepare for her immediate wedding with Don Sancho. In the later scenes the King, resolved on a private vengeance for a private affront, decides to have Bustos made away with by some devoted soldier; and at the suggestion of Arias he sends for Don Sancho. The monarch explains that he needs to have a guilty man slain, and gives Don Sancho a written warrant for the deed; but the loyal subject prefers to rely on the royal word, and destroys the authorization, agreeing to slay the man whose name is written in the sealed paper given to him by the King. Don Sancho, left alone, receives a letter from Estrella, telling him that her brother desires them to be married that very day. The soldier is doubly overjoyed, for this is now his wedding morn, and the King has just confided to him a dangerous task. Then he opens the paper to find that the name of the man he is to kill is Bustos Tabera. Horror-stricken, he debates his duty, only to decide at last that he must obey the King's command, kill his best friend and thereby give up his bride. At this moment Estrella's brother enters, and, to his astonishment, Don Sancho forces a quarrel on him. They draw; Bustos is slain; and Don Sancho is led away to prison. Next the spectators are shown Estrella's happiness as she is decking herself for the bridal. But all too soon come the Alcaldes, bearing the body of Bustos, and telling her that the murderer of her brother is the bridegroom she is awaiting. And here ends the second act, wrought to a high pitch of intensity, with sudden alternations of hope and despair.

What happens in the third act may be more briefly indicated. Estrella comes to the King and claims vengeance on the murderer of her brother, — the man whom she herself loves. The monarch (whose passion has now faded as quickly as it had blazed up) gives her the key of Don Sancho's cell, and with it the power of disposing of the murderer as she pleases. Thickly veiled, she goes to the prison, leads her lover forth, and bids him go free. But when he discovers who it is has released him, he rejects his freedom at the hands of the sister of his victim. He returns to his cell, and as he refuses to give any motive for the murder, the civil authorities condemn him to death — altho the King tries to influence the sentence of the Alcaldes, and even thinks he has succeeded, only to be taken aback by their official

which made no formal distinction between tragedy and comedy,—following the medieval practice rather than the doctrine of the Renascence. A play with a tragic climax might have comic incidents and comic characters, just as a play of humorous intention was likely to contain at least one duel with a possibly fatal termination.

In almost every piece we find the *gracioso*, as the Spaniards call the conventional comic servant of the hero, whose task it is to supply fun at intervals and to relax by a laugh the tension of the overwrought situations. Like the modern melodramatists, the Spanish playwrights understood the value of "comic relief," as it is termed to-day. The gracioso has a part of varying importance; sometimes he is a mere clown always trying to be funny and yet having but little to do with the plot; sometimes he is a clever fellow, quick-witted and sharp-tongued and therefore a chief factor in the intrigue; sometimes he serves as a chorus to voice a common-sense opinion as to the superfine heroics of his master,—and this he does at the end of the 'Star of Seville,' for instance; and sometimes, with the assistance of a female partner, he provides in the underplot a parody of the main story of the play. The relation of Sancho Panza to Don Quixote is that of the gracioso to the hero; and indeed there is no better example of the gracioso anywhere than Sancho,—except that the hasty playwrights never gave the gracioso the vital individuality which the genius of the novelist bestowed on Don Quixote's squire. The gracioso is plain-spoken at times, but he is never so foul-mouthed as are not a few of the comic personages in the Elizabethan plays. Indeed, the Spanish drama is distinctly more decent, both in word and in deed, than the English drama which was con-temporary with it.

In Lope's hands the gracioso was more easily witty than in Calderon's, just as Lope's lighter pieces were more gracefully humorous than were those of his great follower. Lope was naturally gay and seemed to improvise laughter-provoking intrigues, whereas Calderon laboriously con-structed his humorous situations, with skilful certainty, no doubt, but with little spontaneity. The fun of Calderon's 'House with Two Doors' is indisputable, but it is rather mechanical when contrasted with Lope's playful comedy, the title of which in English would be the 'Dog in the Manger.' Here Lope revealed a delicacy of per-ception into feminine psychology; his heroine is a true woman, whereas his hero is a pitiful crea-ture, finding a father by fraud; and in the author's bringing about the marriage which ends the play, we have another instance of the careless cynicism and of the moral obtuseness which accompanied the religious enthusiasm of the Spaniards.

V

CALDERON accepted the several dramatic species which Lope de Vega had devised for his own use,— just as Shakspere took over Marlowe's formula in his youth and in his maturity borrowed Fletcher's also. But Calderon modified scarcely at all the framework his predecessor had prepared. In general his craftsmanship is more careful than Lope's,— altho his expositions are inferior, being often huddled into a long speech or two, as artificial almost as the prologs of Euripides or Plautus, whereas Lope's opening scenes are marvels of clever presentation, taking the spectators immediately into the center of the action.

After the plot is once set in motion Calderon has a more vigorous grasp of his situations than Lope, and a stronger determination to get out of them all they contain of effect. Not only is his technic more conscious and more artful, but also his nature is richer, whereby he is enabled to pierce deeper into his subject; he is more of a poet than Lope. Inferior in comedy, he is superior in tragedy, in his vigorous handling of themes of terror and horror, of supernatural fantasy and of ghastly gloom. Incomparable in his invention of somber situations, he is ever what Lowell called him, an "Arab soul in Spanish feathers."

His plots are unfailingly romantic, even tho there are realistic touches here and there in his drawing of character,— as, for example, in that fine, bold drama of the 'Alcalde of Zalamea,' in which the peasant-judge has a grim humor of his own.

Calderon's acceptance of the tenets of his church was quite as unhesitating as Lope's, and his religion was even more ardent. But his faith was medieval in its narrowness; and this sadly lessens the final value of the plays in which he sought to embody spiritual themes. Altho he reveled in the supernatural, his views of the other world seem now as childish as Marlowe's; and the mind of the Spanish playwright was incapable of any such philosophic speculation as we find more than once in the English poet's 'Doctor Faustus.' Even in his ecclesiastical dramas intended to be performed in the streets on Corpus Christi day, the so-called sacramental-acts,—which were religious masques, descended from the medieval miracles and moralities,—Calderon inclines to make the allegory unspeakably obvious, to bring the mysteries of religion down to plain matter-of-fact, and in short to produce the concrete out of the abstract.

Yet his spectral muse inspired him in the composition of more than one very striking play, on subjects charged with spiritual suggestion. One of these is the 'Devotion of the Cross'; and another, quite as direct in its disclosure of the medievalism of the Spanish, is the 'Wonder-working Magician.' In this latter we are made acquainted with Cyprian, a young student of Antioch, who burns with unholy passion for a Christian maid, Justina. To possess her he sells his soul to the Devil, writing the dire compact with his own blood. The Devil gives the student a year's instruction in necromancy; and he also sets the powers of darkness at work to seduce the girl. But when at length the Evil Spirit tries to carry off the maid, she proclaims her faith and he has to release her. Baffled by her resistance, the Devil seeks to deceive the student by a phantom. A cloaked figure enters and bids Cyprian follow; but when, supposing he has Justina in his arms at last, he joyfully takes off the cloak, he discovers, to his horror, that he is clasping a fleshless skeleton,—who tells him that "such are the glories of the world!" The student insists on an explanation; and the Evil One has to admit that he cannot keep his bargain since Justina is under the protection of a superior power. It is to this power, therefore, that Cyprian appeals when the Devil tries to bear him away. So the student also becomes a Christian; and he and Justina are united in death, both being burnt as martyrs to their faith.

In these plays Calderon shows himself a true

Spaniard, as Lope was also, of a temperament not reflective but essentially sensuous, satisfied to deal with the externals of the mystery of life and not craving an internal solution. What interested him in a plot was what the personages did rather than what they were; and here we see that the difference between Calderon and Lope de Vega is not in kind but in degree. Both of them deal with situation rather than with character. The fiery young adventurers who woo and seek revenge in Calderon's plays, as in Lope's, are all closely akin; they are first cousins to one another, with a strong family likeness; they are, as Goethe called them, "all bullets cast in one mold," with the same unreflecting bravery and the same sense of honor as something outside of themselves and wholly unrelated to conduct,— "a matter of form rather than of feeling," as Lewes said.

VI

CALDERON is a great playwright, no doubt, and so is Lope also; but it may be doubted whether either of them is truly to be considered as a great dramatist. Striking as are their best plays, loftily lyrical as the language may be on occasion, startlingly effective as the successive situations are, we do not find in them an exquisite harmony and a beautiful proportion of the parts to the whole; we do not thrill with an irresistible appeal to our common humanity; we cannot but be conscious that now and again the story has been twisted arbitrarily for the sake of the incidents; and we fail to feel ourselves swept forward by an inexorable movement toward an inevitable end.

Lope de Vega was the earliest of the host of Spanish playwrights, and Calderon was almost the latest, outliving most of the other dramatic poets who had also revealed surpassing fertility of invention,—Guillen de Castro, to whom Corneille owed the 'Cid,' Alarcon, from whom he borrowed the 'Liar,' and Tirso de Molina, to whom Molière was indebted for the imperishable figure of Don Juan. There had been only two playhouses in Madrid when Lope de Vega began to write for the theater; and before Calderon closed his career there were twoscore. The simple platform which had served at first as a stage had got itself in time some sort of scenery; and it was capable at last of some sort of mechanical effects. In the 'Wonder-working Magician,' for example, the Devil flees away finally on the back of a fiery serpent,— just as Medea at the end of the drama of Euripides is borne off by a dragon; and probably the device whereby this spectacular marvel was accomplished was as elementary and as obvious in Madrid as it had been in Athens.

Lope de Vega was a contemporary of Shakspere; and Calderon survived Molière, who may be called the real molder of the modern drama. Before Calderon's death, Racine had elaborated a tragedy as severe as that of the Greek; but there is no trace of any immediate influence of the French stage upon the Spanish. Even the dramatists of England under Elizabeth responded to the Renascence and profited by it far more than the playwrights of Spain, who refused absolutely to avail themselves of the marvelous model which the drama of the Greeks provided, just as they had rejected also the intellectual liberty which was the precious gift that accompanied the revival of learning. In this refusal and in this rejection we see the reasons why the playwrights of Spain, with all their lyric affluence and all their luxuriance of invention, have left us plays which are almost as medieval in their handling of the larger problems of life as they are in their form.

VI. THE DRAMA IN ENGLAND

I

WHILE the Spaniards were thrusting out the Moors and achieving the national unity which had to precede the extension of their rule over much of Europe and most of America, the English were slowly making ready for that sharp contest with Spain the winning of which was to permit them to expand in their turn. The inhabitants of the British Isles, dissimilar in so many ways from the people of the Iberian peninsula, were like them in their strenuous individuality, in their clear knowledge of what they wanted, and in their unbending determination to achieve the object of their desires; and therefore they also were ripe for an outflowering of the drama. In both countries wide popularity had been attained by the miracle-plays and the moralities, even tho these were often narrative and spectacular rather than truly dramatic — even tho the writers preferred to present the successive incidents of a hero's existence rather than to deal more adequately with the crisis of his career. In both countries the first task of the professional playwrights, when they should come into possession of the theater, would be to compact the rambling story and to concentrate attention upon the more significant incidents. In both countries again, the professional playwrights did not hastily discard the dramatic form which had been devised in the middle ages; they accepted it willingly, and modified it only so far as might be necessary.

That in England more modification was found needful than in Spain was due in part to the different reception accorded to the revival of learning. While the Spanish people had little sympathy with the Renascence and strove to reject it, preferring to cherish the ideals they had inherited from the middle ages, the English people felt the influence of the new movement profoundly; in their own fashion they profited by it; and by it they were made ready for the Reformation, which was as welcome to the stalwart Englishmen as it was abhorrent to the devout Spaniards. Even in the drama the Spanish attitude toward the new learning was almost hostile; and Lope de Vega tells us frankly that, as he wrote solely to please the populace, he locked up Plautus and Terence out of sight while he was at work on a play. But the English attitude, sturdily independent as it was, cannot be called unfriendly. The London play-maker, unawed by any authority and always testing the treasures of antiquity before he took them for his own, was yet ready enough — if he found they had anything to teach him — to learn from the ancients or even from the sophisticated Italians, whom he accepted as true interpreters of the classics. What he borrowed at first might be of little value, — like the ghosts who stalked out of Seneca's sonorous pages to thrill the nerves of the Elizabethans; but in the course of time, not a few of the English playwrights came to appreciate the weight and mass which give dignity and power to the Attic drama. We can discover in several of the most gifted of the dramatic poets who made the reign of Elizabeth so glorious, a readiness to accept a Greek play, not as a model to be copied slavishly, but rather as an example to stimulate nobly. They refused always to submit themselves absolutely to the rigid rules drawn up by the Italian critics; but none the less were they inspired now and again to emulate the direct movement and the harmonious proportion of the Athenian masterpieces.

In England the religious drama had about exhausted its vitality when the secular drama was most abundantly flourishing; and of a truth its work was then accomplished in that it had shown how a narrative could be presented in dialog and in that it had encouraged a wide-spread love of acting, which was likely to call into existence a body of professional players, ready to support properly the performance of a more artistic drama, whenever this should be developed. There was acting everywhere throughout England, under the rule of the Tudors,—acting of miracle-plays by the gilds on Corpus Christi day, acting of moralities in the grammar-schools, acting of comic and legendary episodes on the village-greens. From the amateurs who were thus proving themselves, there were in time recruited little bands of professional performers dependent for their livelihood on their technical skill.

These companies of strollers—like the group of players who came to Elsinore at Hamlet's invitation—had no rich repertory to reward the attention of the audiences that came flocking to see them perform in the town-hall, in the courtyard of the village-inn, or in the open market-place. They may have had a chance scene or two of farcical briskness, perhaps elaborated from a humorous episode in some forgotten miracle-play; and they may have had a fragmentary chronicle-play or a dramatized ballad-tale, like that which Hamlet caused to be acted before the King. They did have certainly what were called interludes, often as didactically dull as the moralities from which these interludes had been derived. One contemporary of Shakspere's has left us the record of a stage-play which, when he was a child, he had seen acted by wandering performers before the mayor and the aldermen of the town.

"The play was called the 'Cradle of Security,' wherein was personated a king . . . with his courtiers of several kinds, amongst which three ladies were in special grace with him; and they, keeping him in delight and pleasures, drew him from his graver consellors . . . that, in the end, they got him to lie down in a cradle upon the stage, where these three ladies, joining in a sweet song, rocked him asleep that he snorted again; and in the meantime conveyed under the clothes wherewithall he was covered, a vizard, like a swine's snout, upon his face, with three wire chains fastened thereunto, the other ends thereof being holden severally by these three ladies who fall to singing again, and then discovered his face that the spectators might see how they had transformed him, going on with their singing. Whilst all this was acting, there came forth . . . two old men, the one in blue with . . . his mace on his shoulder, the other in red with a drawn sword in his hand . . . ; and so they two went along in a soft pace . . . till at last they came to the cradle when all the court was in the greatest jollity; and then the foremost old man with his mace stroke a fearful blow upon the cradle, whereat all the courtiers, with the three ladies and the vizard, all vanished; and the desolate prince starting up barefaced . . . made a lamentable complaint of his miserable case, and so was carried away by wicked spirits. This prince did personate . . . the Wicked of the World; the three ladies, Pride, Covetousness and Luxury; the two old men the End of the World and the Last Judgment."

It was with such barren stuff as this that the strolling actors were trying to amuse the country-folk, altho many plays of a solider substance may have been available, some broader in humor and some more direct in action. Yet even in the performance of so primitive a play as this, there was some scope for acting. The performers were slowly training themselves as best they could, making ready for the personation of characters deeper and subtler than any that had yet spoken English; and thus they were rediscovering the principles of the histrionic art.

II

ACTORS fit for their purpose and audiences both abundant and expectant,—these were awaiting the English poets who, not despising the acted drama, rude as it was, should perceive the possibility of improving it, and who should therefore make themselves masters of it, so that they might slowly lift it to the level of literature. But the earlier dramatic efforts of the men-of-letters were academic rather than popular; and they can have had but small direct influence upon the acted drama. A schoolmaster, for example, familiar with the plots of Plautus, rimed an amusing imitation to be performed by his clever boys in the great hall of the school; and yet this 'Ralph Roister Doister,' despite its copying from the antique, is not without a certain English vivacity of its own. Another scholar, a bishop this time,— if indeed the author of 'Gammer Gurton's Needle' was a bishop,—was responsible for a farce, frank of speech, rank with the flavor of the soil, and full of hearty fun, but not unlike the farces of the middle ages and the broader scenes of the mysteries, that of Mak and the Shepherds, for example. A poet of culture, George Gascoigne, freely Englished a prose farce, the 'Supposes,' which the Italian Ariosto had combined out of Latin material. Two courtiers collaborated in writing 'Gorboduc,' an alleged tragedy of mortal tedium, in which everything that might be of interest is merely narrated and never once shown in action. This undramatic attempt of Norton and Sackville was devised in obvious imitation of Seneca; and it possessed elaborate choruses, preliminary dumb-shows, and rhetorical disquisitions. Nevertheless, unfitted as it was for any stage, it was actually acted — but only in what we may term private theatricals. It was even approved by Sir Philip Sidney, who held it up as a model, altho he was forced to regret that it did not observe the Unities of Time and Place. 'Gorboduc' was distributed into five acts, perhaps because Horace had declared this to be the only proper division — but more probably because Seneca had set the example; and it was written in unrimed iambic pentameter, — in what we know now as blank verse, — which, in the hands of later dramatic poets, was to reveal itself as an instrument of unsurpassable vigor, delicacy, and variety. However poor a thing 'Gorboduc' is in itself, it deserved well in that it bequeathed to us the large framework of five acts and the infinite possibilities of blank verse.

While scholars thus vainly amused themselves with dramatic efforts which were never intended to be performed except by a group of amateurs before an audience of dilettants, the professional actors, banded into little companies, had called into being professional playwrights able to dramatize the stories of the Italian novelists and the themes of the Latin poets, then being translated in quick succession. These theatrical compilers, whose names are mostly unknown to us now and whose pieces have rarely been preserved, cared no more for the rules of the Renascence critics, or for the strict imitation of the ancient dramatists, than did the ignorant spectators before whom their hasty dialogs were to be performed. They gave no thought to theory; they took the theater as they found it; and what they tried to do was to get new subjects to treat in the old way, in the way with which the play-going public had already been pleased. That is to say, these professional playwrights, having no marked dramaturgic capacity, followed the later tradition of the medieval drama, setting on the stage all the incidents of a prolonged fiction, just as the whole story of a saint's life had been shown in a miracle-play. Altho the subjects were no longer religious and altho the performers had no longer any connection with the church, or even with the gilds of craftsmen to whom the church had yielded the acting of the mysteries, the plays performed by the strollers were novel only in their subjects;— they were still medieval in their structure.

But as these wandering performers could not avail themselves of the various spectacular devices which were so helpful in retaining the interest of the medieval spectator, they were thus forced to lay stress especially upon those incidents of the story in which the attention of the audience could be aroused by sheer force of acting. The sudden development of the drama in this period is due

in part at least to the growth of a class of professional actors, replacing the amateurs of the gilds.
These professional actors would soon find the
placid dialog of the medieval theater unworthy
of their growing histrionic ability; and they would
not long be content unless they had expressive
characters to personate and absorbing passions
to portray.   As it is in the conflict of duty and
desire that actors find most scope for the
exhibition of their powers, any increase in the
technical skill of the performers would tend at
once to make the plays written for them more
truly dramatic.

There is always a close connection between
the dramaturgic art and the histrionic.   The player
is ever urging the playwright to provide him with
the opportunity for new triumphs; and the dramatist can ever be confident that the actor will
loyally do all he can to express whatever hight
of emotion the situation may evoke.   One reason
why the medieval drama is as dull as it is, and
as uninteresting, is because the mysteries were
both written and performed by casual amateurs,
deprived even of the example which our professional authors and our professional actors supply
to the amateurs of to-day.   A condition precedent
to the growth of a living dramatic literature is the
specialization of professional playwrights and of
professional actors, dependent for their livelihood

on their mastery of their art, and exercising their craftsmanship in wholesome rivalry with one another.

III

In England when Elizabeth was queen the little companies of wandering actors were greatly increased in number. They had placed themselves under the protection of rich nobles or high officials, whose servants they declared themselves to be. Their membership was as limited as their repertory; and four or five players were sufficient to produce such simple pieces as were then available, each of the performers assuming more than one character, if need be,— very much as all the parts in a Greek play had to be divided among three actors. A slim youth might have to impersonate all the female characters,— and here the English, oddly enough, were more medieval than the Spanish, who had already admitted women upon the stage. They carried no scenery with them, for it is scarcely too much to say that scenery had not then been invented. They took with them only the most obvious properties, perhaps a crown for the king and a couple of swords for a combat, and the like. They wore as rich apparel as they could get, with no thought of its propriety to the time and place of the play itself. Thus lightly encumbered they could rove at will, ready to-day to amuse the guests of a noble gathered in the great hall of the castle, and prepared to-morrow to please the humbler audience that might come together in the village.

In those days the English inn was often a hollow square, with a central courtyard girt with galleries; and here, with the permission of the innkeeper, the strollers would put up a hasty platform around which the country-folk might stand, while the persons of quality could look down from the galleries. In London the performances in places of public entertainment drew such concourses of people that the city authorities were scandalized and strove to forbid them; and as a result the players — who had been wanderers hitherto — were forced to build houses of their own just outside of the municipal limits and to establish themselves permanently. They had no models to go by, and in planning their theaters they gave no thought to the sumptuous edifices that had adorned the chief towns of Greece and Rome. They were used to performing in the courtyard of an inn; and therefore the first theater that they built for themselves was apparently no more and no less than the courtyard of an inn — without the inn itself.

The new building was but a hollow square of about eighty feet each way, open to the sky in the center, and consisting of little more than a quadrangle of galleries, to be divided into "rooms," as they were then called, private boxes as we should now term them, for the accommodation of the more particular playgoers. The whole ground floor was the yard, wherein the solid body of the more vulgar spectators had to stand; and into this yard there was thrust out the stage, a platform perhaps forty feet square. Where the rear gallery ran across the stage there hung an arras, a heavy tapestry curtain, to cut off the space behind, which might be used as a dressing-room. The rear gallery itself, just over the platform, was also made useful, serving as a balcony, a pulpit, a roof, or whatever upper chamber might be called for in the progress of the play. The stage was so spacious that some of the spectators were allowed to sit to the right and to the left, on stools to be hired. There was no curtain to pull up or to pull aside; and there was absolutely no scenery of any kind.

The simplicity of the projecting platform, with its pendent arras at the back and its room in the gallery above available on occasion, the absence of all decoration, leaving the space between the spectators on the stage to represent whatsoever strange sequence of places the playwright might need, — all this was perfectly acceptable to most of the uncritical subjects of Elizabeth. It was not acceptable to the critical Sidney, enamored of antiquity and nourished on the Italian theorists. He protested against a stage on which the scene could seem to change continually simply because there was no scenery to be changed.

Sidney was annoyed that "the player when he comes in, must ever begin with telling where he is; or else the tale will not be conceived. Now shall you have three ladies walk to gather flowers, and then we must believe the stage to be a garden. By and by, we hear news of shipwreck in the same place; then we are to blame if we accept it not for a rock. Upon the back of that comes out a hideous monster with fire and smoke, and then the miserable beholders are bound to take it for a cave; while, in the meantime, two armies fly in, represented with four swords and bucklers, and then what hard heart will not receive it for a pitched field." Sidney's contemporaries were not hard-hearted; and they were ever willing to accept a bare stage as a battle-field and as a cave, as a rock and as a garden, as the castle of Elsinore, as the forest of Arden and as the forum of Rome.

As sharp as Sidney's protest against this violation of the alleged Unity of Place is his protest against the equally flagrant violation of the alleged Unity of Time, when the dramatist unhesitatingly shows us a young couple courting, and then married, and parents of children, who grow to manhood, and who are ready themselves to court and to marry, "and all this in two hours' space." Here again, as in the imaginary changes of scene, we see in the Elizabethan drama the survival of the tradition of the middle ages, with the miracle-play ready to unroll before us the long panorama of a saint's existence. And it is an unfortunate fact that the form of the Elizabethan drama, even in the hands of its master-spirits, is often neither truly ancient in its directness nor really modern in its swiftness; it is medieval rather in its absence of restraint. The form was in fact too loose and too flexible to keep those who made use of it up to a high standard; as Huxley pithily put it, "a man's worst difficulties begin when he is able to do as he likes." In the English drama we cannot but remark a certain jerkiness of the action as the place jumps from one country to another, only to spring back again as suddenly; and we cannot but regret a certain lumbering looseness of structure as the episodes lazily follow one another down through the years. The sprawling story of ' A Winter's Tale ' is far more characteristically Elizabethan than the artful concentration of ' Othello ' and ' Macbeth.'

But the playwrights of those days, like the playwrights of every period when the drama has had a vigorous vitality, were intent on pleasing the contemporary playgoers, and they wasted no thought in vain anticipation of the critical judgment of posterity. If a tragedy or a comedy won the boisterous approval of those who had paid to see it, the dramatists asked no more. They lived in the present; and they were in a hurry, for the demand for new plays far exceeded the supply. So long as the companies of actors were strollers, a very limited repertory had sufficed, and a play might be performed again and again in different parts of the island; but just as soon as the actors were established in London permanently, then there was need of novelty; and if the theaters were to be kept open, a constant succession of new plays was imperative.

The acted drama was scarcely considered as belonging to literature,— indeed, it was held in contempt by many critics. But to write for the theater was almost the only means whereby a man-of-letters could make a living — unless he chose to turn actor also. So it is that we see the clever young fellows, eager to push their fortunes, the fledgling poets, the scholars just out of the universities, joining themselves to the players, some of them becoming actors, but most of them being satisfied merely to furnish the new plays required by the quick rivalry of the London playhouses. They plied as hacks, doing whatever odd jobs they were asked to undertake, now polishing up an old play, then dramatizing a tale from the latest translation, and next collaborating, two or three of them, in a hasty effort to build a gruesome tragedy out of the last murder that had got itself sung in a ballad. Not many of these prentice play-makers were endowed with the dramaturgic instinct, but the few who had the native gift soon had opportunity and practice to attain skill. No doubt the youthful dramatists were aided also by the practical advice of the actors themselves, who knew what they wanted and who were then in a position to insist on getting it. In England under Elizabeth the actors were also the managers of the theaters, or at least the foremost of them were controllers of the enterprise and sharers of the profits, dividing the best parts among themselves and paying wages to their humbler associates. One reason for the extraordinary productivity of the drama just then may be found in this fact, that the management of the several playhouses was chiefly in the hands of the actors; and another cause, even more obvious, can be seen in the sharp competition between the several playhouses.

Within a short time after the opening of these theaters just outside the limits of London, the needful conditions of a national drama were present. There were the playhouses themselves, primitive indeed according to our notions, but perfectly satisfactory to those who attended them. There were the companies of actors, accomplished in their art and ardent for fresh triumphs. There was also the varying population of the capital to supply an unending succession of playgoers of all classes, nobles and gentry, students from the universities, townsfolk, rustic visitors, and seafarers just home from perilous voyages. The English people were never more healthy in mind and in body than they were then, never more adventurous in spirit, never more wilful and self-assertive. These characteristics are favorable for the growth of the drama; and these characteristics are all of them abundantly displayed in the drama that soon sprang up luxuriantly.

IV

THE new play-makers were men of far more ability than the unknown writers in whose footsteps they were following; but they never set themselves up as innovators. They worked in the old tradition cheerfully, trying to provide the players with the kind of play that they knew the playgoers liked. No doubt they wished to better their copy if they could, but they were scarcely conscious that they were really making over anew the art they had inherited from their forgotten predecessors. Like these predecessors, they wrote especially to please the groundlings who stood in the yard, but they sought also not to displease the gallants who sat on the stage. They were better educated, and therefore they could go farther afield, not only for material, but also for effects. From Seneca,— whose Latin plays, never really acted, altho possibly sometimes recited, were the earliest specimens of a persistent and pestilent type, the so-called "drama for the closet," the play not intended to be played (an obvious contradiction in terms),— from the Hispano-Roman rhetorician, they borrowed the practice of frequent murder and the evocation of frequent ghosts. In their heaping up of horrors they were probably encouraged by the contemporary popularity of the Italian novelist, with his constant commingling of lust and gore. The laxly knit chronicle-play was soon stiffened into the so-called tragedy-of-blood, a dramatic form which was very pleasing to the Elizabethan audiences and which was tempting even to Shakspere himself.

While a true tragedy should purge the soul with terror, the tragedy-of-blood was satisfied to thrill the nerves with horror. A necessary figure in the conduct of such a play was a ghost who proclaimed the duty of revenge and who, in anticipation, gloated over every bloody stroke of vengeance. The author charmed the eyes of the spectators with combats, hangings, tortures, dumb-shows, and masques, while also he tickled the ears of the audience with vehement phrases and high-sounding bombast. And yet, however coarse may seem the art of this tragedy-of-blood, it was at least alive, which could be said of very few of the miracle-plays. As it dealt with the clash of passion against passion it was essentially dramatic, which the chronicle-plays at first were not. However violent the crudities in the early 'Spanish Tragedy' of Kyd, and whatever the flagrant faults of taste and structure in the later 'Duchess of Malfi' of Webster, there is no denying the vigor of these plays nor their exceeding vitality. They were planned to be acted then and with no thought that they would ever be read now. They were devised to hit the taste of the London playgoer of those unsettled days, and they achieved this purpose amply. In so doing the tragedy-of-blood helped and hastened the coming of the true tragedy which was to supersede it.

Thomas Kyd was not the only predecessor of Shakspere by whose labors the great dramatist was to profit. While Kyd was showing how to knit a plot and how to heap up situations tempting to energetic actors, his friend Christopher Marlowe was helping to transform the shapeless chronicle-play. If in 'Hamlet' Shakspere was at first following Kyd's lead, in 'Richard III' he was treading in the footprints of Marlowe. Kyd is the more dextrous playwright, no doubt; but Marlowe is the more gifted poet, with a deeper insight into human motive. Marlowe it was in whose hands blank verse revealed itself as an incomparable instrument for the dramatic poet; and Marlowe it was who showed how to search the soul of man in more than one notable passage in more than one of his pieces.

But his best-known play, 'Doctor Faustus,' proves that he was not a born play-maker, instinctively grasping the essential struggle and unfailingly presenting it in the necessary scenes. The play was little more than the mere slicing into dialog of the old story-book; and only in a chance speech here and there did Marlowe appear to apprehend the full philosophic value of the suggestive theme he had chosen to treat. Now and again he seemed to get to the heart of the matter and to voice his vision with unfailing felicity of phrase; but for the most part he was content to make a use of the supernatural which is not unfairly to be called puerile, just as the comic passages are almost childish. Among the characters were the Good Angel and the Evil Angel and the Seven Sins, all survivals from the earlier moralities, and serving to show how close the connection was between the medieval drama and

the Elizabethan.   As a humorist Marlowe is pitiful; as a playwright he is frequently feeble; as a
creator of character he is often deficient; but as a
poet he holds his own with the best.   As a poet,
indeed, he may even boast that he had Shakspere
for a pupil. Justly has his mighty line been
praised for its power and its nobility, for its delicacy and its exquisite modulation.

While Marlowe with his 'Edward II' was setting a model for the splendid series of Shakspere's
histories, and while Kyd was complicating the
ghastly plot of the 'Spanish Tragedy,' which
was to serve as a stepping-stone to the great
tragedies of Shakspere, other young spirits were
lighting up the path leading to the realm of fantasy, where romantic-comedy best could flourish.
In the medieval drama the scenes intended to be
amusing were sometimes truly humorous, with a
shrewd homeliness of phrase and a direct realism
of character-drawing; but most of them were
trivial and coarse and dependent for their immediate effectiveness rather upon horse-play than
upon genuine humor.   The free adaptations
which later scholars had made from the Latin
and from the Italian possessed plots more artfully
put together; and sometimes the plays had acquired a certain simple flavor of the soil to which
they had been transplanted.   But not in the
boisterous scenes of the miracle-plays, not in the

ingenious imbroglios of the Italian or of the Latin, was there any worthy model for a truly English comedy; and yet in the earlier attempts at romantic-comedy the influence of all three of these can be traced, accompanied by a large contribution from the contemporary English novel, itself derived indirectly from the pastoral-romance of the Continent.

The comedies of John Lyly, 'Endymion' and its fellows, seem to us to have literary merit rather than dramaturgic effectiveness. They appear to us too artificial to hit the taste of the town, too distended with labored allusiveness; but before an audience of courtiers they were performed more than once and with some measure of approval. In these contemporary allegories ingenious equivoke brought about pleasantly playful situation, characters were sketched lightly yet with piquancy and freshness. The dialog with all its insistent antithesis was often witty — altho not quite so often as the author labored to make it. There was a gentle suggestion of gracious courtliness in the atmosphere of these comedies of Lyly's not to be perceived in any earlier plays — a gracious courtliness which is to be found later in full flower in 'As You Like It' and 'Twelfth Night.'

In its main theme Robert Greene's 'Friar Bacon and Friar Bungay' recalls Marlowe's 'Doc-

tor Faustus' with its naïf handling of the supernatural; but the underplot sets forth a story of
young love triumphant over circumstance; and
we have here another source of romantic-comedy,
with its fresh love-making in the open air, as
prettily pastoral as one could wish, tho it was
also only doubtfully dramatic.   Indeed, even in
his plays Greene revealed himself rather as a
novelist, with a graceful lyric note of his own.
None the less he had advanced a step beyond the
courtly Lyly, a step nearer to that kingdom of
romance which was to call itself Verona or Illyria
or Bohemia, a desert· country by the sea, where
exiled dukes were to roam the lonely forest and
where lovely heroines were to disguise themselves
as lads.   In his treatment of English rural life,
with its plain-spoken and free-handed English
folk, in his contrasting of fantasy and reality, in
his commingling of quaintly humorous characters
with figures of pure imagination, Greene is a pre-
cursor of Shakspere, to be held in remembrance
not so much for what he actually accomplished
himself as for what he prepared and made possible.

V

GREENE and Lyly, Marlowe and Kyd, had all of
them aided the advance of the English drama
from out the monotonous formlessness of the

medieval pieces; and they had all striven to devise the kind of play most likely to hit the taste of the Elizabethan playgoer, with his sturdy body, his free spirit, and his alert mind. Then a dramatist more gifted than any of the four came forward to profit by what they had done. This newcomer was no theoretic reformer; he had no artistic code already formulated; he was simply a practical playwright who happened also to be a great poet. Shakspere's first labors were humble enough, merely the patching of old pieces, whereby he learned the secrets of the craft. Even when he started to write plays of his own there was no overt effort for novelty. He began where the others had left off, as might have been expected from a capable young fellow who sought to earn his daily bread by preparing plays to suit the existing conditions of the theatrical market,— plays intended first to tempt the actors to perform them and then to tempt the spectators to applaud and to come again the next time the comedy or the tragedy or the history might be announced for repetition.

But even in this prentice work there was evidence that the young hack-writer had an individuality of his own. Better than any of his groping predecessors could he use situation to reveal character and find fit expression for feeling and for thought at the moment of crisis. His earliest plays were little more than imitations; and in 'Love's Labor's Lost' he was almost as artificial as Lyly, altho he was at once closer to life and far cleverer. 'Titus Andronicus,' wherein horrors on horrors' head accumulate, was simply a tragedy-of-blood on the model of Kyd's most popular play. The 'Comedy of Errors' was only a farce with an ingeniously mechanical plot, and yet redeemed by more than one character of a true humanity. In 'Richard III' the disconnected episodes of a history were artfully knit into a certain unity by the incisive presentation of the royal villain. In few of these earliest plays was there any hint of audacious ambition;—indeed, all that the author was aiming at was a chance to earn his living while learning his trade. He was not yet sure of himself or of his audiences.

"Steeped in humor and fantasticality up to its very lips, the Elizabethan age," so Matthew Arnold tells us, "newly arrived at the free use of the human faculties after their long term of bondage, and delighting to exercise them freely, suffers from its own extravagance in this first exercise of them, can hardly bring itself to see an object quietly or to describe it temperately." Shakspere was a true Elizabethan and he had his full share of this fantasticality and of this intemperance. These characteristics are most paraded in the earliest plays, but they are not absent from the latest, in not a few of which we cannot but note a careless playfulness at times and a reluctance to be bound by any restraint that irked him. The austere perfection of Sophocles was not his ideal; yet when he chose and when the theme he had chanced upon happened to arouse all his powers, he revealed the possession of a constructive faculty not inferior to the great Greek's. When his interest flagged, as for example in 'All's Well that Ends Well,' he might let his story loiter as languidly as it was wont to do in the old chronicle-plays; or when his subject might be unworthy of him, as happened now and again, notably in 'Measure for Measure,' he failed to exert himself.

But when his imagination kindled at his theme and he put forth all his strength, it was with unerring certainty that he pierced to the center of the subject and that he presented in action one after another the needful scenes, — the *scènes à faire*. 'Romeo and Juliet' and 'Julius Caesar,' 'Macbeth' and 'Othello,' are plotted with conscious art and consummate skill. They are each of them plays of a wonderful unity of construction. Each has a marvelous beauty of form, being exquisitely proportioned as a whole and carefully wrought in all its parts. These plays, conceived for performance in the little cockpit, which the Elizabethan theater was, with a bare platform projecting into the yard, with no scenery and no propriety of costume, with the women's characters impersonated by shaven boys, with the gallants smoking on the stage, and with the groundlings restless in the yard,— this 'Othello' and this 'Macbeth' are truly as architectonic as the stately Attic tragedies, which were performed in the spacious Theater of Dionysus before the cultivated Greeks.   These English tragedies have a solid simplicity of their own, not Greek indeed, but of a kind which the open-minded Greek would have been able to appreciate.   They meet the requirements laid down by Aristotle quite as well as the best plays of the Athenian tragic writers — altho not quite in the same way.   The Greek perfection has been defined as " fit details, strictly combined, in view of a large general result nobly conceived"; and even this perfection Shakspere attained now and again.   He attained it, indeed, whenever he took the trouble to do his best.   He attained it in 'Hamlet,' which is outwardly a mere tragedy-of-blood, with its revenge and its ghost and its final massacre, but which is inwardly the eternal tragedy of the human soul at war with inexorable circumstance.

The absence of the chorus and the consequent removal of any limitation of time allowed the English dramatist to avoid the fixity of character imposed upon the Greek, who could deal only with the culmination of his action. Shakspere achieved almost his highest triumph in the revelation of character as it slowly disintegrated under stress of repeated temptation. We can behold the virus of ambition working in Macbeth, and we are made witnesses of the persistent solicitation of his wife. We are shown how the poison of jealousy slowly destroyed the nobility of Othello's nature. The conditions of the Greek theater made it impossible for Sophocles to attempt this; and he had no time allowed him even to suggest the certain change in the character of Oedipus after the hideous catastrophe.

Here at least the later poet could profit by his larger liberty, altho the absence of all restriction permitted him the unduly distended action of 'A Winter's Tale,' and the slovenly huddling together of incidents in 'Cymbeline.' Rarely indeed does even the foremost of the English dramatists take the trouble to seek the simplicity of form and the solidity of structure which even the least of the Greek dramatists was ever striving for, altho without always achieving. Here we see how the highly trained Athenian audiences helped to hold the Greek dramatic poet up to a lofty standard; whereas the London audiences, eager and tumultuous and uncultivated, exacted nothing from the English dramatic poet, except that he should deal with life directly and forcibly.

Shakspere was not only the foremost of English dramatists: he was also a practical man of affairs, clear-headed and self-possessed; and it is not to be wondered at that he did not often exert himself more than was needful. He did not write his plays for publication and for posterity: he wrote them to be acted in the theater in which he was a sharer; and for the most part he seems to have been satisfied when they pleased the playgoers and brought in large audiences. But he was also a great artist, with the great artist's sensual enjoyment of the dextrous exercise of his technical skill; and thus it was that from time to time a rich theme would waken his ambition to go far beyond any demands of the Elizabethan spectators and to work out an imperishable masterpiece, which would move his contemporaries, no doubt, but which would also carry a message to later generations — a message his contemporaries may not even have suspected.

But it was on the audience of his own day that he kept his eye steadily; and he gave them what he knew they relished, the coronations and processions and stately spectacles they were amused by, the combats and battles they delighted in, the ghosts and the witches they believed in, even if he himself did not. He had imagination beyond other men, but he had also common sense in the same superlative degree. He had his head in the clouds at times, but he always kept his feet firm on the ground. An idealist, as a poet must be, he was a realist, as a successful playwright always is. He was never remote or unfriendly or retiring; indeed, all the records remind us that he was hearty in his friendships and that he gave himself freely to his associates. He had broad human sympathy; and, altho apparently rather aristocratic in his political opinions, he could fellowship with common men; and perhaps this is why common men did not fail to understand him then, and indeed often understand him now better than the more dainty and the supersubtle.

He was not over-squeamish, and he never shrank from plain speech. But he was clean-minded beyond most of his fellow-playwrights of those spacious days; and in his attitude toward women he was a gentleman, even in his comedies,—whereas men of far better breeding, Beaumont and Fletcher, for example, were frequently dirty in thought and often foul in phrase. His manners were better than those of the contemporary men-of-letters, and so also were his morals. There was in his plays no silly practice of so-called "poetic justice"; for anything so petty Shakspere's vision was too broad and his insight too piercing. But neither was there any paltering with the law of life nor any extenuation of wrong-doing. The sinner has ever to pay the dread reckoning at last, even tho it is only by himself that he is called to account. Shakspere's philosophy was sound all through, and so was his ethical code, even tho it is unformulated. The moral might not be tagged to the fable, but only the wilfully blind could fail to find the lesson. Shakspere did not think it wise to crystallize his morals; rather were they held in solution, to be tasted and felt, not seen or measured.

Perhaps this was specially evident in the histories, that grand gallery of full-length portraits, in which the long line of English kings step one by one from out the dull annals and start into life, illumined by the inner light of imagination. But it was evident also in the joyous group of poetic comedies, creations of airy and capricious fantasy, in which the poet peopled a world of exquisite unreality with figures of eternal truth and beauty. What were 'As You Like It' and 'Twelfth Night' but pure romances shown in action with young lovers wooing wittily, moved rather by pretty sentiment than by any unplumbed depth of passion? Just as other dramatists had relieved a story of terror with scenes of lively humor, so Shakspere, in 'Much Ado about Nothing' and in the 'Merchant of Venice,' sustained the comedy, which was his chief interest here, by underplots so serious that they might seem almost tragic.

For these delightful fantasies we have no other

term than comedy; and yet nothing can be more
remote from what we ordinarily understand by
the word. "Romantic-comedy" we must call
it, and of this romantic-comedy Shakspere was
the undisputed master. Contemporary life is the
stuff out of which the comedy-of-manners is
wrought; and to contemporary life Shakspere
seems scarcely to have given a thought. The
only play of his in which he dealt avowedly with
the men and women of his own time and of his
own country was the ' Merry Wives of Windsor,'
which was, in effect, only a farce, since the situations of the story determined the characters.

Yet altho Shakspere gave no thought to contemporary life, it is true also that he never sought
to represent anything else. He was no historical
novelist to attempt the impossible; and the lovers
of the 'Merchant of Venice,' the men of the
watch of 'Much Ado about Nothing,' the mob
of ' Julius Caesar,' and the courtiers of 'Hamlet,'
are all of them English, and all subjects of the
Virgin Queen. They were first of all human
beings, set in special circumstances of time and
place; and then they were also Elizabethans, with
all the vigor, the humor, and the whim of the
men and women whom Shakspere knew as boy
and man in country and in town. Because
Shakspere neglected the comedy-of-manners,
his fellow-playwrights could not climb unaided
to the lofty level of high comedy. For romantic-

comedy, as for tragedy and for history, he had set a pattern, and the others were able to work in accordance therewith. But for the modern comedy-of-manners men had to wait for Molière to supply a model which should endure for centuries.

VI

YET the foremost of Shakspere's fellow-playwrights was also a master of the comic. Realistic as was the humor of Ben Jonson, and sometimes almost sordid in its details, it could on occasion rise splendidly on the wings of imagination — like the humor of Aristophanes, of Rabelais, of Mark Twain, all of them interpretative realists. Often, indeed, the humor of Ben Jonson strikes us now as arbitrary and as adamantine. The characters he brought forth on the Elizabethan stage were richly realized and unforgettably individualized; but they were frequently as rigid as a Greek masque. They lacked the flexibility and the moderation of human nature. If the comedy-of-manners is the result of the clash of character on character, the comedy-of-humors is rather the result of the clash of caricature on caricature. But however exaggerated their characteristics,—and this very exaggeration was an integral element of Ben Jonson's comic power, as it was also of Smollett's and Dickens's,— the persons of his plays had indisputable vitality.

They took part in a plot built as solidly as the Pyramids, and as massively planned. Coleridge was right in likening the framework of the 'Alchemist' to the structure of the 'Oedipus,' for Jonson's comedy, like the tragedy of Sophocles, had a beginning, a middle, and an end; and it was wholly devoid of everything which did not help to bring about the ultimate recoil of the intrigue. There was conscious art here, a technical mastery of which the stalwart poet was openly proud. And proud he was also of his scholarship, of the immense variety of his information, of the load of learning he could carry with ease, even making it serviceable in his comedies. In his tragedies this scholarship weighed him down and stiffened his muscles. In his more serious plays he was less felicitous and less fortunate than in his comic dramas. His tragedies were put together with the same integrity of workmanship; but they seemed to lack something, some sweep of passion to stir the blood, or some touch of elemental simplicity to move the heart. Jonson knew books as well as any of his contemporaries; and his comedies proved that he knew men also. Women he did not know so well,— or else, like other broad humorists, he did not greatly care to portray their pettier frailties.

Women are more important in the plays of

Beaumont and Fletcher, poets of a lighter weight
and of a more romantic temperament. Many of
their pieces can scarcely be classed as comedies,
since they contained scenes of searching emotion
and scenes of boisterous humor, often so loosely
conjoined that there is no saying whether the
serious or the comic plot is the more important.
In more than one of their dramas it would be
very difficult to discover any real unity of action.
But laxly as Beaumont and Fletcher may have
put their plots together, they had not a little dramaturgic dexterity. They had caught the knack of
story-telling on the stage; they had an instinct
for an effective situation; and they could sketch
a daring character likely to take with the spectators. Altho far inferior to Ben Jonson in comic
force, they had a pleasant sense of humor and a
pretty turn of wit. They rarely rose to any
hight of passion or even of pathos, yet they had
sentiment at least and lyric grace.

They could be courtly, as became men of good
breeding; but they sometimes sank into blatant
vulgarity not only of phrase but of thought.
Here they were on the level of their contemporaries, a level to which Shakspere rarely descended. Perhaps it was due to the fact that all
the women's parts were acted by young men
that the Elizabethan playwrights delighted in un-
clean innuendo; and yet this was a temptation that

Shakspere rarely felt. Shakspere's women are ever womanly; they are eternally feminine; and altho not without a frankness no longer in fashion, they are essentially pure-minded. But if Shakspere is cleaner than his contemporaries, Beaumont and Fletcher are not worse sinners than the other playwrights, the most of whom were ready enough to pander to the baser portion of the Elizabethan audience. It was to the better element of this Elizabethan audience that Beaumont and Fletcher more often appealed. They deserved the favor that they received by a succession of lively plays, cleverly calculated to please the prevailing taste, plays with picturesque action, with abundant fun, with ingenious episodes, and with occasional scenes of genuine force.

Other playwrights there were a-plenty in the later days of Elizabeth and the earlier days of James; some of them were merely poets, who wrote for the stage because the theater then offered the best chance of self-expression, and some of them were true playwrights, gifted with a genuine dramaturgic instinct. Ford and Webster were gloomy souls in revolt, combining horrors wilfully; they were poets of strange power, rather than playwrights; and they turned to the dramatic form, not from any native impulse, but rather because the demand for plays coincided with their own pecuniary needs. Heywood, on the other hand, was a born play-maker, and his 'Woman Killed with Kindness' remains a jewel of simple pathos. Massinger was another, a master of flexible blank verse; and in his powerful comedy, 'A New Way to Pay Old Debts,' there was a bold etching of a malevolent character, Sir Giles Overreach, so actable that it kept the stage for more than two centuries. Middleton, again, and Dekker had their share of success, altho much of their humor is made according to the accepted stage-formula of the Elizabethan theater. Shirley also, the latest of them all, had his full share of strength, altho he lacked sympathy and tolerance, and altho his humor is without ease or unction.

"Genius is mainly an affair of energy," said Matthew Arnold, "and poetry is mainly an affair of genius." Energy the Elizabethan dramatic poets had in superabundance; and what they lacked, many of them, was restraint and order and harmony. Shakspere towered above them all in power, in genius, in poetry,—and also in art, in self-control, in elevation of purpose, and in dramaturgic craftsmanship. And they and he were closely akin; all were children of the race and of the time. "There are the same characters in their dramas as in Shakspere's," so Taine declared, "the same violent and terrible characters, the same murderous and unforeseen occurrences, the same sudden and frenzied passions, the same irregular, capricious, turgid, magnificent style, the same exquisite poetic feeling for rural life and landscape, and the same delicate, tender, affectionate ideals of woman."

VII

No epoch in all the long history of the drama is emblazoned with more glorious names, not even that which was made resplendent by Aeschylus, Sophocles, and Euripides, by Aristophanes and Menander. In sheer force, even the Greek drama might be held inferior to the English. Where the Athenians regained their superiority over the Elizabethans was in art, in the conscious purpose held steadily until its accomplishment, in the subordination of parts to the whole, in the subduing of individual freedom to a larger symmetry. Some of Shakspere's plays, but only too few of them, were wrought with consummate care; and so were many of Ben Jonson's; but for the rest what is often most evident now is the waste and misdirection of energy, the unwillingness to husband genius, the wilfulness that is almost freakishness.

Behind these wanton defects was a medieval uncertainty of form; and here was the chief cause of the deficiencies of the English drama at the moment of its most splendid expansion. Its form was inadequate, largely because the Elizabethan theater had advanced so little beyond the theater of the middle ages. The English drama was less medieval than the Spanish drama, which was its brilliant contemporary; for it had freed its spirit, at least, and it had an open mind. It had even been aided in its development by the influence of the Greek masters, altho mainly through their Roman imitators — an influence far less felt in Spain. None the less was the presentation of a play of Shakspere's quite as medieval as the presentation of a play of Lope de Vega's; it was almost as primitive as the presentation of a mystery just before the Renascence. The performance took place on a mere platform, in the open air, with most of the turbulent spectators standing on three sides; and the large majority of these spectators were likely always to be men of low breeding and of coarse tastes. Altho a dramatist must needs appeal to the plain people, to his contemporaries as a whole, and not to any upper class or cultivated caste alone, yet he is unfortunate if there is not among the spectators enough education to leaven the mass. It was a misfortune that the Elizabethan theater was so rude a thing; it is to be regretted that public opinion allowed the dramatist not merely needful liberty of form but also unlimited license of structure; and it was doubly unfortunate that

VII. THE DRAMA IN FRANCE

I

WHEN the church gave up to the laity the control of the mysteries, and the vernacular of each of the several peoples was substituted for the uniform speech of the clergy, then there began to be a divergence which did not cease until the drama in each of the modern languages was strikingly representative of the racial characteristics of those who spoke that tongue. Indeed, there is no art in which national traits are more clearly revealed than in the drama,— not only in what is said and done on the stage, but also in the very form of the play itself.

From the common stock of the mystery, universal throughout medieval Europe, Spain evolved a type of drama quite different from that evolved in England during the same centuries; and the Spanish play with its ingenious surprises, and the English play with its energetic directness, are not more sharply differentiated from each other than each of them is from the

French play with its decorous reserve and its psychologic subtlety. The French followed the bent of their own genius, just as the Spanish had done, and the English; and this led them in time to a drama not so energetic as the English and not so full of surprises as the Spanish, but surpassing them both in the symmetry of its structure and in the logic with which its action was conducted. The narrowness of form which became in time one of the most marked peculiarities of the French drama was no doubt due mainly to the French liking for restraint, to a hereditary preference for rules of guidance; but it was also caused, in some measure, by the circumstances of the evolution of tragedy in France out of the miracle-play.

When the mystery was turned out of the French churches, it erected out of doors and in the public square its long platform, with a row of mansions at the back to suggest the more necessary of the successive places where the episodes of the gospel-narrative were to be shown in action. In Paris, the miracle-plays being at last intrusted to the control of the Brotherhood of the Passion, a band of burghers united for this special purpose, there was no change in the method of representation when the performances were taken indoors once more and established in the Hôtel de Bourgogne.

Just as the earliest English theater was copied
from the courtyard of an inn, because the strolling actors were accustomed to that, so in France,
and for a like reason, the earliest theater was
modeled on a tennis-court. It was long and
narrow; and it had a shallow platform at one
end. This stage was decorated with such unrelated mansions as the play might require; and
its limited space must have been as badly
crowded as the chancel of the church had been
when the original stations began to multiply in
number.

The disadvantage of this massing of many
places all at once on the stage would be greatly
increased when the well-known Bible story and
the legends of the saints, almost equally familiar
even to the spectators who might see them for
the first time, ceased to supply the sole material
for the anonymous dramatists, and when chronicle-plays began to be made out of the semi-
legendary lives of heroes and out of the wholly
fictitious romances of chivalry. A throne under
a canopy was enough to suggest the palace of
Herod, if the playgoer already knew that such a
king had once reigned; and so a gate in a wall
would serve for Jerusalem if the audience was
already aware that a part of the action would
take place in that city. But when fictitious heroes, absolutely unknown to the public, had un-

heard-of adventures in wholly imaginary castles and cities and forests, and when these unfamiliar castles and cities and forests were all huddled upon the stage at once, each of them not actually represented but merely hinted at,— a tower for the castle, a gate for the city, a tree or two for the forest,— then was chaos come again.

It was in the neutral ground surrounded by these emblems of various places that the actors played their parts, the castle or the city or the forest, each in its turn, being used for their entrances upon the stage; and yet it seems as if these shorthand indications of the several localities would be more likely to confuse the spectator than to aid him in realizing the successive scenes. Awkward as this arrangement may have been, it was an inheritance from the medieval theater; and the tradition was so firmly rooted that this composite set was the only stage-setting familiar to the French playwrights until the middle of the seventeenth century. Not only did the earliest of French dramatists, Hardy, conform to it; but even the first plays of Corneille were conceived in accord with its conditions.

Only the more serious drama was thus encumbered with a complicated stage-setting. The comic drama was free from any vain effort of this sort; its action took place in the neutral ground,— that is to say, on the bare stage, with

only a curtain at the back, for so the strolling
players had been accustomed to present a farce
on an improvised platform in the market-place.
Even during the Renascence personal and political satires got themselves acted now and again;
but the staple of the humorous stage was still
the farce with its sturdy fun and its practical
joking. Not a little of the national ingenuity in
handling a situation logically, and in extracting
from it the utmost of its theatrical effect, is already
revealed by these early comic dramatists of
France, unknown for the most part, writing
directly for the common people, often vulgar,
never squeamish, and liberal of Gallic salt rather
than of Attic wit. Comedy of a high elevation
the French were to wait for, till their native stock
had been cross-fertilized by Spanish example.
For many years after the Renascence had brought
about a new birth of the other arts in France,
the drama, serious as well as comic, did not respond to its influence, and remained medieval
both in its manner and in its matter.

In these days of dawning promise, the French
men-of-letters, like the Italian men-of-letters a
little earlier, detested the medieval theater and
despised it. They admired antiquity; and they
sought to imitate the dramatists of Athens and of
Rome, altho they really preferred Seneca to
Sophocles. They persuaded themselves that one

of their number had written a play when he had merely prepared a poem in dialog, often protracted by the needless introduction of a chorus in the manner of the Greeks. But no one of these French men-of-letters, whatever his value as a poet, was in fact a playwright; and in these poems in dialog there was little or nothing of the truly dramatic. There were no contending passions, no character in the fell clutch of fate, no struggle firmly set forth, no *scène à faire*. Declamation there was in abundance—words, words, words; and indeed what plot there might be served chiefly to bring in a variety of topics for rhetorical treatment or for lyrical expansion. A monolog sometimes filled almost a whole act; and the personages did not converse together,— they delivered lectures to one another.

In these frigid specimens of oratorical verse there was neither character nor action to reward the effort of professional actors; and this is an added reason why they were performed only by amateurs, by the poets themselves and their comrades, before audiences of their friends and admirers. These chilly imitations have a certain importance in the history of French literature; but they are quite insignificant in the history of the French drama. Mere poems in dialog, presented by amateurs before dilettants on chance occasions, could have little influence upon the actual theater of the time; and it is only in the actual theater of the time, however primitive and rude it may be, that any advance in dramaturgic art can be made. The development of a dramatic literature is always dependent upon an already existing organization of players in a playhouse with playgoers accustomed to a certain traditional way of presenting plays. Just as the practice of building houses of some sort necessarily goes before any growth in the art of architecture, so an actual theater is a condition precedent to a living dramatic literature.

No improvement of the drama, no refining of its art, has ever been accomplished by a poet, however gifted, who scorned the actual theater of his own time and failed to master its methods. Improvements are wrought only by those who are intimate with all the conditions of the object to be perfected. But pressure from the outside has often been beneficial to the theater; and by merely literary criticism the professional playwright has sometimes been stimulated to a loftier ambition. Perhaps the professional playwright may even have found his profit in a study of the alleged plays in which the poets failed to carry out adequately the ideas they advocated. And this is what seems to have happened in France toward the end of the sixteenth century, when the Brotherhood of the Passion leased their theater in Paris to a company of professional actors who had been performing in the provinces in plays written for them by their own hack-dramatist Hardy.

II

THE Parisian playgoers were accustomed to the long-drawn action and to the plain-spoken humor of the miracle-plays and of the dramatized romances devised according to the same formula. Hardy accepted this formula fully, composing his plays to suit a stage decorated with as many mansions as his story might call for. But he was a born playwright; and he had learned by long experience in the provinces how to hold the interest of an audience. He had more of the dramaturgic faculty than any of his predecessors, the most of whom, indeed, had had very little. In his hands the loose chronicle-play was stiffened into consistency and its action was concentrated to bring out more boldly the dramatic passages in which the actors who employed him could most forcibly display their ability. He could evoke character out of situation, altho, for the most part, his psychology was but summary. For situation itself he had an instinctive feeling like that of his English contemporary

234

Kyd; but he lacked Kyd's rhetorical fervor. He was not a poet himself, yet he was prompt to profit by what the poets had written, both by their precepts and their practice. Like Kyd. again, he put his plays in five acts, in accordance with the example of Seneca and the advice of Horace. He was led in time to devise the species of play which came to be known as tragi-comedy and which kept its popularity through the first half of the seventeenth century.

This tragi-comedy of Hardy's served as the connecting-link between the medieval drama and the true tragedy which was later to be illustrated in France by Corneille and Racine. This true tragedy was slowly evolved out of tragi-comedy, as tragi-comedy had been slowly evolved out of the chronicle-play. Hardy availed himself of the rimed alexandrines, which he had found in the unactable plays of the poets who had vainly essayed to revive the classic drama,—just as Kyd and Marlowe had accepted the unrimed iambic pentameter of 'Gorboduc'; and thus Hardy helped to establish the rimed alexandrine as the verse to be employed thereafter by French dramatic poets. Hardy's own poetry deserved no high praise; but it was more pretentious than any yet spoken in the actual theater. His plays appeared to have a certain literary flavor because he drew freely upon the ancients for his plots, upon Vergil, for example, and more particularly upon Plutarch; and this may have made some of his pieces seem almost classic, in spite of the fact that his treatment of these stories was frankly contemporary.

It was probably due to Hardy that people of culture became interested in the drama of the day, and that men-of-letters started to write for the actual theater, accepting its conditions unhesitatingly, and striving to give it a more literary atmosphere. More than one court-poet ventured to prepare plays to be acted by the company of the Hôtel de Bourgogne; and the upper circles of society were led to attend the performances, altho until then ladies had absented themselves from the theater, in consequence of the coarseness and the vulgarity of the customary entertainment. The frequent presence of women of rank in the playhouse helped along the purifying of the contemporary drama in which the younger poets were engaged. Society was settling down after long years filled with feuds and factional intrigues; and, with stability and peace, manners were softened and taste was improved. The theater began to be recognized as an important element of social life even before Richelieu took it under his high protection, ambitious himself to win acceptance as a dramatist. In time a second playhouse was opened in the Marais; and the

236

actors who managed this were eager to welcome any novelty which would aid them in their rivalry with the older company.

To supply these two playhouses there sprang up a generation of dramatic poets, following in the footsteps of Hardy, altho they possessed less of the native play-making gift. They were more declamatory than he had been, and not so direct; they were more affected in the conduct of their stories and in the suggestion of the motives of their characters. No one of them equaled Hardy in sturdy common sense or in ingenious construction. And while he had invented his plays himself, making use of materials supplied by epic and by history, they began to borrow their plots ready-made from the dramatists of Spain and Italy. At the same time they imported also the so-called "rules of the theater," which had been elaborated in Italy by the critics of the Renascence, and which had been rejected by the practical playwrights of Spain and England. In France these rules met with a different fortune; they slowly established themselves in the literary drama; and they shackled the French stage until early in the nineteenth century.

In Spain and in England the playwright had seen no advantage in fastening these fetters on his limbs; and in neither country did the playgoers puzzle themselves about any theory of art or any code of rules so long as the playwright was able to hold their interest, to amuse their eyes, and to startle their nerves. They made no cavil at any license the dramatist might take, so long as he gave them the special pleasure which they expected from the theater. It is a necessary condition of this enjoyment in the playhouse that the spectators shall understand at all times what is shown before them on the stage; and here we have an explanation of the apparent anomaly that the Three Unities were welcomed by the play-going public of Paris, altho the play-going public of Madrid and of London had been wholly indifferent. In Paris the adopting of the Unity of Place would abolish the clutter of incongruous mansions which the stage of the Hôtel de Bourgogne had taken over from the outdoor platform of the miracle-plays. These mansions must have been difficult to distinguish one from the other on the dimly lighted stage; and, so far from aiding the imagination of the audience, they may have kept the attention distracted during the earlier passages of the play.

How confusing this medieval scenic device might be may be guessed when we learn that in one play of Hardy's the stage was set with a palace at the back ; while on one side there was the sea, with a ship having masts, on which a woman appeared, and from which she threw herself into the water; and on the other side there was a fine room having in it a bed decked with its sheets. Almost as complicated was the stage-setting requisite for one of the early plays of Corneille, the 'Illusion Comique,' where a richly decorated palace was in the center, with a park on one hand, and on the other a cave for a magician on the top of a mountain. It is small wonder that the audience would welcome a simplification of such a stage-setting as this, and would gladly advocate any theory the application of which would result in getting rid of a complexity so bewildering.

Also to be allowed full weight is the fact that the French are not so individual as the Spaniards, nor so self-willed as the English. Rather are they governed by the social instinct, relishing strict order, not to say restraint. Inheritors of the Latin tradition of decorum, the French do not dislike rules, nor do they really object to what might seem to the English to be restrictions. Above all are they fond of logic, and of the simplicity which comes of having a single aim; and so far as the acceptance of the rules of the theater and the adoption of the Three Unities helped their playwrights to attain this end, it was beneficial to their dramatic literature. But if we may judge by the history of the theater elsewhere, we can be certain that the French play-going public would never have approved of the demand of the literary critics for the Three Unities, if the underlying principle of the rules had not been acceptable to the genius of the race.

III

CORNEILLE, the first of French dramatic poets, possessed his full share of this national characteristic; and he displayed it plainly in the earliest of his more important plays—in the 'Cid,' which was derived from a Spanish drama written by one of the followers of Lope de Vega. Hardy had already shown him the way of condensing the ordinary medieval narrative in dialog into a succession of striking adventures; and Corneille in turn concentrated all his effort on a single main situation, the very climax of a struggle between desire and duty. He cut out of his Spanish original, and cast away, all that did not serve to throw into higher relief this final exercise of the human will, always the dominating element of a true drama; and thus it was that he fixed once for all the form and the content of French tragedy.

The popularity of the 'Cid' with the playgoers of France was immediate; and it has been enduring. No tragedy is more attractive in Paris to-day after almost three centuries; and in the first flush of its novelty the rush to see it was so insistent that seats were set upon the stage. The custom thus introduced into France was already established in England; and it must have increased the tendency toward scenic simplicity, since the sides of the stage were not thereafter serviceable. Yet the 'Cid' itself had been devised in accord with the conditions prevailing at the time it was written; and when it was originally produced at the theater in the Marais the stage was arranged to represent simultaneously the dwelling of Chimène, the apartment of the Infanta, a public square, and the council-chamber of the King. Half a century later this cumbrous complication had disappeared, and the play was performed in a room with four doors,—that is to say, in a neutral ground, perhaps suggesting the public square, but having immediate access to the quarters of the King, of the Infanta, and of Chimène.

Founded on a loosely constructed Spanish drama, and written to suit the conditions of the French theater as Hardy had modified them, the 'Cid' did not exhibit the Three Unities; and for this dereliction it was censured at Richelieu's command by the French Academy, which he had founded to be the custodian and the controller of taste. Corneille defended himself as best he could; and in his later plays he sought to avoid giving to the partisans of the Italian theories any occasion to find fault with him. The final establishment of the rules was really due to Corneille's avowed adhesion to them and to his obvious effort to conform. But he himself was never at ease within the limitations which he had felt himself forced to accept. They irked him painfully; they cramped his bold spirit; and he was continually striving to argue himself out of them or to interpret them into harmlessness. Sometimes, it may be, the necessity of wrestling with the difficulty helped him to a more concise and a more vigorous expression;—the history of every art abounds in instances of an obstacle which the artist, after trying in vain to get around, has at last been able to use as a stepping-stone to a higher achievement.

Quite possibly this was the case with his tragedy of 'Horace,' in which his power as a dramatic poet is displayed amply and characteristically. The theme was tempting to a man of his temper; it was the conflict between family affection and fervid patriotism. The play was as simple in plot as it was swift in action, the poet presenting only the naked climax, stripped of all accessory episodes. In this directness of movement he was aided by his submission to the rules; and on this occasion the observation of the Three Unities called for no sacrifice. The single plot is presented at its culmination in a single day; and the stage represents a single place,—a room in the house of old Horatius in Rome. The first act begins with the entrance of Sabina, with her friend Julia; Sabina is an Alban; and Alba is at war with Rome. She is at once the sister of the three Curiatii and the wife of one of the Horatii. She declares her divided feelings, and then departs, after Camilla enters. Camilla is a Roman; she is the sister of the three Horatii; and she is beloved by one of the Curiatii. She has been to consult an oracle; and she has been told that the war will end this very day, and that she and her lover will then be united, never to part. Then the Curiatius she loves enters, to inform her of a truce and of a proposal to leave the war between the two cities to be decided by a combat of three champions chosen from each side. Elated by this good news, they depart,—and the leaving of the stage without any actors was taken by the audience as notice that the act was ended. As there were spectators seated at the sides of the stage, it is probable that no curtain was lowered.

The second act opens with the entrance of Curiatius and Horatius, and the former congratulates the latter that the three Horatii have been chosen as the Roman champions. Then a friend appears to announce that the Albans have named the three Curiatii to defend their cause. Horror-stricken as they are, the young men do not shrink from the deadly duty, altho Camilla comes on to beg her lover to withdraw as best he can. Soon Sabina appears to urge her brother not to flinch, even tho his hand is armed against her husband's life. Finally the father of the Horatii steps forward to reveal himself also as a model of noble austerity. He has the last word, bidding the young men do their duty and leave the rest to the gods. In the third act we are made sympathizers with the suspense in the Roman household while the brothers are fighting three against three in front of the hostile armies. Sabina wishes for the success of her brothers, while Camilla is ardent for the triumph of her lover. The elder Horatius enters to attest again that honor is ever to be held dearer than life; and when Julia brings the dread news that two of his sons have been killed, while the third has saved himself by flight, the father grieves not at the deaths of the two but only at the cowardice of the one. In the fourth act the old man's shame is turned to pride when he is told that the flight of his surviving son was only a device to separate the three opponents, whereby the Roman was able to face them singly and to slay them one by one. Camilla hears the fatal news in silence, but when her brother returns, glorying in his victory, she breaks forth in violent imprecations against Rome, the cause of her lover's death,—whereupon her outraged brother pursues her off the stage and slays her with the sword that slew the man she loved. In the fifth act he is accused before the King; and it is her father who justifies his deed. At last the monarch pardons the murder because of the victory that went before.

The dramatic interest of 'Horace' is as indisputable as that of the 'Cid.' Indeed, we have here the drama reduced to its essence, the stark assertion of the human will, the shock of contending passions, the collision of conflicting duties. The situation at the center of the story is very unusual, not to say most extraordinary; and this is one reason why Corneille liked it. But when once it was granted, he made little further demand upon the indulgence of the spectators; he proceeded to handle his theme with sober logic and to extract from it both pity and terror. Corneille's characters are larger than life; they are of heroic size, all of them, men and women; and they breathe a rarer air than everyday mortals. But they are consistent with themselves and with one another. Their exaltation of sentiment may seem to some of us a little too high-strung, yet it was to them perfectly natural; and to the French audiences of the seventeenth century it was more than acceptable: it was stimulating and satisfying. The Parisian playgoers thrilled with pleasure then, as they do now, when the characters vied one with another in voicing noble sentiments always perfectly phrased.

For Corneille was no mere playwright, skilled in building up a plot: he was also a true poet, altho very unequal; and he was a passed master of versification. His lines have the double merit of polish and vigor. He could compact the expression of his emotion into a pregnant word or two; or, when he preferred, he could express it at length in stately and sonorous couplets, over-emphatic at times, no doubt, but rarely open to the reproach of pomposity.

IV

RACINE, who followed Corneille as Euripides followed Sophocles, took over the form of tragedy which the elder poet had marked with his own image and superscription, altho the younger poet modified it in some slight measure to suit his own powers and his own preferences. Corneille had been over-lyric at times, altho he had been far less epic than any of his predecessors as a playwright; Racine was more rigorously dramatic. Accepting the limitation imposed by the Three Unities, which were in accord with his temperament, Racine condensed still further the themes he treated. He focused the attention upon fewer figures; and he simplified again the action until English critics are wont to deem his plays bare and cold, altho in fact a fire of passion is ever glowing within them. He was an adept in construction; and his plots, narrow as they may be, are exquisitely proportioned, revealing consummate art in the conduct of the story. He avoided scrupulously all digressions and underplots and parasitic episodes.

The extraordinary situations that Corneille had been delighted to discover in history, Racine rejected altogether, choosing rather to deal with what was less extravagant,— the growth of a man's love for a woman who loved another, or the consequences of a woman's mad passion for a youth who cared nothing for her. In his plays, as often in Corneille's, the action is internal rather than external; and the moral debate within the heart of man is not always accompanied by mere physical movement, visible to the heedless spectator. Racine did not seek to interest the audience in what his characters were doing before its eyes, but rather in what these characters were in themselves, and in what they were feeling and suffering. He was an expert playwright, as well as a master of psychologic analysis; and this is why he was able to accomplish the difficult feat of making his study of the inner secrets of the human soul effective on the stage. His story might be slight, but in his hands it was always sufficient to express tensity of emotion and to command abundant sympathy.

In the tragedy of 'Andromaque' the spectator is made to see how Pyrrhus, son of Achilles, is about to abandon his promised bride Hermione, daughter of Helen, because he is desperately enamored of Andromache, widow of Hector. On behalf of the Grecian chiefs, Orestes, son of Agamemnon, appears to demand of Pyrrhus the sacrifice of the son of Hector and Andromache. Orestes loves Hermione, who loves the faithless Pyrrhus, who longs for Andromache, who is devoted to her husband's memory. To save her son, Andromache weds Pyrrhus, resolved to slay herself as soon as the boy's safety is assured. In the agony of her jealousy, Hermione hints to Orestes that she will be his, if he will slay Pyrrhus before the wedding with Andromache. But when Pyrrhus is killed and Orestes comes to claim his reward, Hermione recoils with horror and reproaches him for his evil deed; and then she rushes forth to put an end to her own life upon the bier of the man she had loved in vain. The death-dealing blows are never given before the eyes of the spectators; and yet this artistic reticence results in no loss of interest, since the attention of the audience is directed, not to the mere doings of the characters, but to the effect of these doings, first upon Hermione and then on Orestes.

Racine's conscious possession of the power of

arousing and retaining the interest of the playgoers of his own nation in his minute discrim-
ination between motives and emotions, may be
one of the reasons why he was prone to choose
a woman as the central figure in most of his
plays; and here again is a point of resemblance
to Euripides. Racine was led also to make use
of love as the mainspring of his action, partly,
perhaps, because the passion of man for woman
had not often been considered by Corneille,
and partly because this was of all the passions
the one he himself best understood. A loving
woman Racine could always delineate with delicate appreciation and with illuminating insight.
His touch was caressingly feminine; whereas the
tone of Corneille was not only manly but ever
stalwartly masculine. Corneille, argumentative
as he was at times and even declamatory, was
forever striving to fortify the soul of man, while
Racine, with a softer suavity, was seeking rather
to reveal the heart of woman, to lay it bare before us, palpitating at the very crisis of passion.
As we gaze along the gallery of Racine's fascinating heroines, we observe that desire often
conquers duty; but when we call the roll of
Corneille's heroes, we behold men curbing their
inclinations and strong to do what they ought.

Thus it may be that Racine was the nearer to
nature, since it is often a strain upon the spectator

unaccustomed to it. This impression of artificiality is deepened by Racine's enforced employment of the conventional vocabulary of gallantry
to express sincere and genuine emotion. It was
the misfortune of Corneille also that he had to
deal with the universal in terms of the particular,
and that his plays, like Racine's, were conditioned
by the sophisticated taste of the playgoers before whom they were performed. If we contrast
the courtly audiences of Racine with the gathering of Athenian citizens to judge a drama of
Sophocles, and with the spectators of all sorts
thronging to applaud the plays of Shakspere,
we can see one reason why French tragedy lacks
the depth and the sweep of the Greek, and why
it has not the force and the variety of the English. French tragedy appeared, as Taine has told
us, "when a noble and well-regulated monarchy,
under Louis XIV, established the empire of decorum, the life of the court, the pomp and circumstance of society, and the elegant domestic phases
of aristocracy"; and French tragedy could not but
disappear "when the social rule of nobles and the
manners of the antechamber were abolished by
the Revolution."

V

IF the manners of the antechamber were the
cause of the self-consciousness we cannot but

remark in French tragedy, on the other hand the empire of decorum was a government under which French comedy could come to its fullest perfection. Molière, younger than Corneille and older than Racine, is greater than either, partly because of his own superior genius and partly because the racial characteristics of the French can find their fullest expression rather in comedy than in tragedy. Indeed, Molière is not only the foremost figure in all French literature: he is also one of the three great masters of the drama, worthy to be set by the side of Sophocles and of Shakspere.

Altho Molière came at the moment of maturity, when the methods of the medieval theater were modified finally in conformity with modern conditions, it was only very slowly that he attained to a complete understanding of his genius or to a recognition of its limitations. He was an actor, like Shakspere, and the manager of a company of comedians who had wandered for years about the provinces and who had settled themselves at last in Paris. His earliest attempts were but trifles, brisk and broad, in the manner of the Italian comedy-of-masks, mere comic imbroglios with no pretense of literature to sustain their very practical joking. Even the brilliantly written comedy of the 'Étourdi' is as fantastic as these farces of the Italians, and almost as mechanical in the ingenuity of its expedients. Not until after he had established himself in Paris did he bring out the ' Précieuses Ridicules,' in which he first touched the real life of his own time. It was only a comedietta, but it was based on a solid observation of his contemporaries; and its success encouraged him to seek subjects in the society he saw about him. This is the very material that Shakspere never cared to deal with; and Molière made it the staple of his work.

Altho his position as the manager of a company of actors led him to return frequently to the Italian formula with its easy extravagance and its liberality of laughter, Molière slowly enlarged his manner as he felt his footing firmer. He brought forth a series of comedies of a steadily increasing depth; and as he became more accustomed to handling the realities of life, his characters were more boldly drawn, his plots were less arbitrary, and his themes took on a profounder meaning. But he was no mere man-of-letters with a purely theoretic philosophy of life: he was a practical playwright, master of all the resources of the theater of his own time. As a school-boy he had studied Latin comedy, and he knew all that Plautus and Terence could teach. He was nourished on the succulent humor of the old French farces, with their hearty

fun and their pertinent sketches of character.
He had spied out the secrets of the Spanish playwrights, fertile inventors of amusing situations.
He had absorbed every device of the Italian
comedy-of-masks with its incessant liveliness
and its ingenuity of intrigue.

By years of acting as a stroller in the provinces
he had taught himself how to hold the attention
of the illiterate audience while he was unfolding
his plot and while he was carrying on his story.
By bitter experience he learned that a play, however lofty in design or however poetic in expression, is nothing, and less than nothing, if it cannot
please contemporary playgoers. Timidly at first
and tentatively, he began to put something more
into his plays than mere amusement. He began
to impart a serious meaning to the comic drama.
He began to use his comedies to express his own
feelings and his own opinions about the structure of society and the conduct of life. He recognized that as a comic dramatist it was his duty,
first of all, to make the spectators laugh; but he
was able skilfully to enlarge his manner so that
he could also make them think even while they
were laughing. He had an imaginative insight
into the absurdities, the frailties, the petty faults,
and the lesser vices of human nature. What he
observed he reflected upon; and he related it to
the larger outlook on human nature which was

his also; and when he reproduced upon the stage what he had seen in the world his social satire was informed with the shrewdest common sense, and it was sustained by abundant and exuberant humor, by a power of compelling laughter unequaled among all the moderns.

It was this penetration of Molière's humor into the secrets of our common humanity, combined with his mastery of the technic of the theater, so that there was ever a perfect adaption of the means to the end, which has made his comedies the final model of that " picture of life which is also a judgment." The humorist was a moralist, as all great humorists have been; and he had, moreover, the melancholy which is ever the accompaniment of a profound humor. His nature was really richer than Racine's and deeper than Corneille's, and his vision of life was more piercing; and therefore the range of his comedy was far wider than the range of their tragedy. Indeed, he exercised himself in more different species of the drama than any other of the great dramatists. Shakspere is versatile enough, with his histories and tragedies and romantic-comedies and farces. But Molière is even more multifarious. He attempted pure farce, the ' Médecin Malgré Lui '; the comedy-of-intrigue, the 'Étourdi '; the comedy-of-manners, the ' École des Femmes '; the comedy-of-character, the ' Avare '; romantic-comedy, the 'Amphitryon'; tragi-comedy, 'Don Garcie'; comedy-ballet, 'Monsieur de Pourceaugnac'; criticism in dialog, the 'Critique de l'École des Femmes'; satiric interlude, the 'Impromptu de Versailles'; legendary drama, 'Don Juan.' No one has ever handled comedy in its various aspects so brilliantly and so broadly as Molière; and he has left us in the 'Femmes Savantes' the incomparable model of pure comedy at its highest and best, while he presented us also with the type of comedy sustained by philosophy in the 'Misanthrope,' of comedy gently relaxing into farce in the 'Bourgeois Gentilhomme,' and of comedy almost stiffening into drama in 'Tartuffe.'

No one of Molière's comedies is more characteristic than 'Tartuffe,' more liberal in its treatment of our common humanity, braver in its assault upon hypocrisy, or more masterly in its technic. And the technical problem was as difficult as the theme was daring. Bringing before us a man who uses the language of religion as a cloak for the basest self-seeking, Molière devised his situations so artfully that the spectators can discount the villain's fair words, and that they know him for what he is, even before he makes his first appearance. The opening scenes deserve the high praise of Goethe; and indeed there is no more adroit exposition in the history of the drama. Two acts are employed to set before us the family relations of the credulous Orgon, into whose confidence the unscrupulous Tartuffe has wormed himself. We are made acquainted with Orgon's second wife, with his old mother, with his son and his daughter, and with the whole household.

Tartuffe does not appear until the third of the five acts; and by that time the audience is ready for him and able to see through him at once. His projects are plain, even if they are somewhat contradictory—as the plans of a villain often are. He is seeking to capture Orgon's wealth for himself, to marry Orgon's daughter, and at the same time to seduce Orgon's young wife. However he may disguise his foul purpose beneath pious phrases, the spectators are never in doubt as to his true character; and he has no need of any aside to elucidate his motives. Never does he lower the mask, as Iago so often does, or lay his soul bare in soliloquy. Once we think he has been caught and is about to be exposed; but again he wins over Orgon by the very extravagance of his self-accusation. Once more he is led actually to betray himself, making love to Orgon's wife with Orgon concealed under the table. And then when he sees that he is found out at last he stands forth brutally and claims the house as his under a deed of gift. Furthermore, he denounces his benefactor as implicated in a political intrigue; and Orgon finds himself in a pitiful situation with total ruin impending. At the very end of the play, when there seems to be no way out of the difficulty, Molière most artfully unties the knot by the intervention of the King, Louis XIV himself, who is made to exert his arbitrary power to free the foolish Orgon and to send Tartuffe to prison.

Before Molière wrote, French comedy had been excessively romantic in manner, with its plots fabricated out of adventures and accidents, and with its personages of tradition and fantasy. Molière brought comedy back to reality. He dealt directly with life as he beheld it about him. He set upon the stage the men and women of his own time, a wonderful collection of portraits,—vital, vigorous, and undeniable in their veracity. In this splendid series of comedies the age of Louis XIV starts again into life, with all its decorum, its social ease, its hardness of heart; we are permitted to visit the court and the town, and to make acquaintance with the nobles, the burghers, the physicians, the actors, and the men-of-letters, with the lackeys, the serving-maids, the young girls, the prudes, and the coquettes.

We can see Molière's wholesome sympathy with youth and love; we can note his kindliness and his common sense; and we cannot help remarking his ever-growing detestation of affectation and of pretense. In all his larger comedies the dominant note is sincerity, a scorching scorn for sham and humbug, a burning hatred of hypocrisy. He is honest himself and frank; his satire is never mean or malevolent; his attack is always open and direct. His hearty laughter clears the air; and we love him for the enemies he made. Now and again, it may be admitted, his tone is hard; and it must be acknowledged further that he rarely softens into pathos. Indeed, of pathos, which is generally the inseparable accompaniment of humor, Molière had almost as little as Aristophanes. What he had instead of pathos was melancholy,—a puissant and a searching melancholy, which strangely sustains his inexhaustible mirth and his triumphant gaiety. Sometimes, while we are laughing at the sheer fun which envelops his broader comedies, we are allowed to catch a glimpse of his inexpressible sadness which is at the core of his humor.

Molière is superior to Corneille and to Racine in the variety of his themes, in the breadth of his philosophy, in the ingenuity of his technic; and in spite of the fact that he is a writer of comedies while they both wrote tragedies, and that he did not always use verse, he can be called a greater poet than either of them, — if we may give to the word poet its larger meaning. To us who speak English the rimed alexandrine is a rhythm too artificial and too complicated to be perfectly satisfactory in the drama; and to many of us French itself is not a poetic language. But even if the French are somewhat lacking in the energetic imagination which ought to inform tragedy, they have special qualifications for comedy. They are easily witty; they are inventively humorous; they have a sharp sense of the ridiculous; they are governed by the social instinct. It is natural enough that the greatest of comic dramatists should be a Frenchman, and that we should owe to Molière the final form of comedy. Quite possibly the form of comedy which Molière established in French is very like that which Menander had devised for his own use in Greece two thousand years earlier; but however probable the suggestion may be and however alluring, there is no proof of it available now, since the plays of Menander are lost to us forever.

Not with Menander is Molière to be measured, and not with Corneille and Racine; his place is rather with the supreme masters of the drama, with Sophocles and with Shakspere. In pure comedy his supremacy is as indisputable as that of Shakspere both in romantic-comedy and in tragedy, and as that of Sophocles in tragedy alone. He may be the least of the three, perhaps; but he is the latest also. He has this one advantage over his predecessors: he is not so far distant from us as they are. The society he has depicted is more like the world we are familiar with. Above all, the theater for which he wrote is almost the same as ours.

It was the special good fortune of Molière that he came forward as a dramatist at the very moment when the circumstances of a theatrical performance had already assumed the aspect to which we are nowadays accustomed. Whereas the plays of the great Greek dramatist were prepared to be performed outdoors in a hollow of the hills without either stage or scenery, and whereas the plays of the great English dramatist were intended to be produced in a theater without a roof and on a stage without scenery, the plays of the great French dramatist were written to be acted in a theater properly roofed and illuminated by artificial light, and having a stage supplied with scenery. In the masterpieces of Sophocles we can see the ancient form in its most consummate perfection, strange and remote as that may seem to us to-day; and in the masterpieces of Shakspere, mighty as was his genius, we cannot but perceive the disadvantage of the form he had to use, a form which

261

was almost medieval and which was disesta-
blished even in England only a few years after he
withdrew from active labor as a playwright.
But in the masterpieces of Molière we have a
form which is indisputably modern and perfectly in accord with the conditions of the theater
at the beginning of the twentieth century. The
plays of Sophocles and of Shakspere cannot be
shown on the stage of to-day without many
suppressions and modifications; but the plays
of Molière can be performed now anywhere
without change or excision, absolutely as they
were acted by their author and his comrades
nearly two hundred and fifty years ago. So far
as the external form of their dramas is concerned, Sophocles is ancient, Shakspere is medieval, Molière is modern; and the large framework of his ampler comedies has supplied a
model for the dramatists of every living language.

VIII. THE DRAMA IN THE EIGHTEENTH CENTURY

I

EVERYWHERE in Europe the modern drama has been evolved from out the drama of the middle ages; but the development had been slower in France than in Spain and in England; and this retarding of its evolution was fortunate for the French, since the golden days of their dramatic literature arrived only after the conditions of the theater had become far less medieval than they had been during the golden days of the Spanish and of the English dramatic literatures. It was natural that the more modern form of play should be taken as a model by the poets of the other countries, the more especially at the beginning of the eighteenth century, when the French were everywhere accepted as the arbiters of art, the custodians of taste, and the guardians of the laws by which genius was to be gaged. In England the Puritans had closed the places of amusement and had thus broken off the theatrical traditions that ran far back into the middle ages; and when the playhouses opened again after the Restoration, the managers had to gratify new likings which king and courtiers had brought back with them from France. Even tho the plain people in London continued to prefer the plays of Shakspere to belauded adaptations from Corneille or Racine and to icily decorous imitations like the 'Cato' of Addison, and even tho the plebeian folk in Madrid still relished the plays of Lope de Vega and Calderon, the English men-of-letters and the Spanish men-of-letters were united in taking an apologetic tone toward the earlier dramas which had pleased their less cultivated forefathers. In England as in Spain the learned critic was willing to admit that these earlier dramas had a certain rough power which might move the uneducated, but he had no desire to deny that they wanted art. For instance, Doctor Johnson, when he brought out his edition of Shakspere in the middle of the eighteenth century and when he ventured a timid suggestion that possibly the so-called rules of the theater were not absolutely infallible, seems to have felt almost as tho he was taking his life in his hands.

In Italy and in Germany, as in England and in Spain, the men-of-letters maintained the necessity of conforming to the theatrical theory of the

French, because they believed the French to be the only true exponents of the Greek tradition, which it was the bounden duty of every dramatic poet to follow blindly. The rules of the theater as the French declared them had only a remote connection with the Greek tradition; and they consisted mainly of purely negative restrictions. They told the dramatic poet what he was forbidden to do, and they declared what a tragedy must not be. To accord with the demands of the French theory a tragedy should not have more or less than five acts and it should not be in prose; it should deal only with a lofty theme, having queens and kings for its chief figures, and avoiding all visible violence of action or of speech, and all other breaches of decorum; it should eschew humor, keeping itself ever serious and stately, and never allowing any underplot; and, above all, it should permit no change of scene during the whole play, and it should not allow the time taken by the story to extend over more than twenty-four hours.

These were the rules to conform to which Corneille cramped himself and curbed his indisputable genius, with the result that he is to Shakspere " as a clipped hedge is to a forest,"— to quote an unsympathetic British critic. A certain likeness to the virgin woods is discoverable in the Elizabethan drama, whereas the drama of

Louis XIV resembles rather a pleasure-park laid out by some such architect as Lenôtre. French tragedy had a graceful symmetry of its own, but it was lacking in bold variety and in imaginative energy. Here is an added reason why it was widely acceptable in the eighteenth century, which has been termed " an age whose poetry was without romance" and " whose philosophy was without insight." The century itself, rather than the French example, is to blame if it has left so few poetic plays deserving to survive. What Lowell called " its inefficacy for the higher reaches of poetry, its very good breeding that made it shy of the raised voice and the flushed features of enthusiasm," enabled the century to make its prose supple for the elegancies of the social circle and for the literature which sought to reflect these elegancies. " Inevitably, as human intercourse in cities grows more refined, comedy will grow more subtle," so De Quincey declared; " it will build itself on distinctions of character less grossly defined and on features of manners more delicate and impalpable."

II

A FLEXIBLE prose is plainly the fittest instrument for the comedy-of-manners; and the comedy-of-manners is as plainly the kind of drama best suited to the limitations of the eighteenth century. By their comedies rather than by their tragedies are the dramatists of that century now remembered. Their comedies, like their tragedies, were composed in imitation of French models; but the influence of Molière was as stimulating as the influence 'of Corneille and Racine had been stifling. Within a few years after Molière's death the type of comedy which he had elaborated to suit his own needs and to contain his own veracious portrayal of life as he saw it, had been taken across to England by the comic dramatists of the Restoration, some of whom had borrowed plots from him and all of whom had tried to absorb his method. No one of the English dramatists had Molière's insight into character, or his sturdy morality. Congreve and Wycherley, Farquhar and Vanbrugh helped themselves to Molière's framework only to hang it about with dirty linen. At times Molière had been plain of speech, but he was ever clean-minded; whereas the English dramatists of the Restoration were often foul in phrase and frequently filthy in thought also.

Clever as these Restoration comedies were and brilliant in their reflection of glittering immorality, their tone was too offensive for our modern taste, and scarcely one of them now survives on the stage. Yet the form they had copied from Molière they firmly established in England, where the conditions of the theater had come to be like those in France; and this form has been accepted by all the later comic dramatists of our language, who have never cared to return to the looser and more medieval form which had to satisfy the humorous playwrights under Elizabeth. Steele and Fielding and, later in the century, Goldsmith and Sheridan continue in English comedy the tradition established by Molière. In ' She Stoops to Conquer ' and in the ' Rivals ' there is an element of rollicking farce not quite in keeping with the elevation of high comedy but not unlike the joyous gaiety which laughs all through the ' Bourgeois Gentilhomme.' In the ' School for Scandal ' we have an English comedy with something like the solid structure of the ' Femmes Savantes,' but narrower in its outlook, not so piercing in its insight, and far more metallic in its luster.

The English followers of Molière are many, but they are not more numerous or more amusing than those who in his own country profited by the example he had left. Regnard is almost the equal of his master in adroitness of versification and even in comic force, in the power of compelling laughter. ' Monsieur de Pourceaugnac ' has hardly added more to the mirth of the French than has the ' Légataire Universel.' But

Regnard is fantastic and arbitrary in the conduct of his plots; and he lacks the truth to life and the penetration which characterize Molière. Lesage comes nearer, in his knowledge of human nature and in his appreciation of its frailties, altho it is in his novels rather than in his plays that he reveals himself most fully as a disciple of Molière. Like Fielding in England, Lesage in France carried over into prose-fiction the method of character-drawing which he had acquired from the greatest of all comic dramatists.

In the 'Dépit Amoureux' and in the 'École des Femmes' Molière had shown how to set on the stage certain more delicate phases of feminine personality; Marivaux pushed the analysis still further, thereby enriching French comedy with a series of studies of women in love, — women at once ethereal, sophisticated, and fascinating. Broader than Marivaux was Beaumarchais, broader and franker; his psychology was swifter, his action was more direct, and his stagecraft was more obvious. It was 'Tartuffe' and the 'Étourdi' that he had taken as his models, but he was only clever and wily where Molière was transparently sincere; and instead of the large liberality of the dramatist under Louis XIV the dramatist under Louis XVI had a caustic skepticism. The career of Beaumarchais was as varied in its vicissitudes as that

of his own Figaro; he was an adventurer himself, like Sheridan, his contemporary on the other
side of the Channel. The 'Barber of Seville'
was as lively and as vivacious as the 'Rivals';
and the 'Marriage of Figaro' was as scintillating
and as hard as the 'School for Scandal.'

There was a disintegrating satire in these
comedies of Beaumarchais, a daring bitterness
of attack like that of a reckless journalist who
might happen also to be an ingenious and witty
playwright. Where Molière had assaulted hypocrisy in religion and humbug in medicine,
Beaumarchais made an onslaught on the Ancient
Régime as a whole. No doubt a portion of the
vogue Beaumarchais enjoyed among his contemporaries was due to their covert sympathy
with the thesis he was so cleverly sustaining on
the stage. He knew how to profit by the scandal aroused by his scathing insinuations against
the established order. Yet he was not dependent on these factitious aids, and his solidly constructed comedies reveal remarkable dramaturgic
felicity. They have established themselves
firmly on the French stage, where they are still
seen with pleasure, altho certain polemic passages here and there strike us now as extraneous and as over-vehement. Beaumarchais is the
connecting-link between the French comedy of
the seventeenth century and that of the nineteenth, between Molière and Augier.

III

ALTHO the French theorists insisted on a complete separation of the comic and the tragic, disapproving fiercely of any humorous relief in a tragedy, they also maintained that comedy should hold itself aloof from vulgar subjects, that it should ever be genteel; and there were some who held that it ought to be unfailingly dignified. Even in England Goldsmith was reproached for having disfigured 'She Stoops to Conquer' with scenes of broad humor "too low even for farce"; and Sheridan in the prolog of the 'Rivals' felt forced to make a plea for laughter as a not unnatural accompaniment of comedy. Without asserting categorically that the drama should be strenuously didactic, many critics considered that it was the duty of comedy, not first of all to depict human nature as it is with its foibles and its failings, and not to clear the air with hearty laughter wholesome in itself, but chiefly to teach, to set a good example, to hold aloft the standard of manners and of morals. Dryden had declared that the general end of all poetry was "to instruct delightfully"; and not a few later writers of less authority were willing enough to waive the delight if only they could make sure of the instruction.

Thus there came into existence a new dramatic species, which flourished for a little space on both sides of the English Channel and which was known in London as sentimental-comedy and in Paris as tearful-comedy, *comédie larmoyante*. The most obvious characteristic of this comedy was that it was not comic; and in fact it was not intended to be comic, but pathetic. It was a mistake that a play of this new class should call itself comedy, which was precisely what it was not, and that by this false claim it should hinder the healthy growth of true comedy with its ampler pictures of life and its contagious gaiety. But the new species, however miscalled, responded to a new need of the times. It was the result of that awakening sensibility of the soul, of that growing tenderness of spirit, of that expansion of sympathy, which was after a while to bring about the Romanticist upheaval.

In England this sentimental-comedy never amounted to much, even tho it had for one of its earliest practitioners Steele, who claimed that a certain play of his had been " damned for its piety." But Steele, undeniable humorist as he was, lacked the instinctive touch of the born playwright, and his humor was too delicate to adjust itself easily to the huge theaters of London. Steele's is the only interesting name in all the list of writers for the English stage who intended to edify rather than to amuse and who did not regret that their comedies called for tears

rather than laughter. That the liking for sentimental-comedy was more transient in England
than in France perhaps was due to the fact that
the Londoners had already wept abundantly over
dramas of an irregular species, not comedies of
course, nor yet true tragedies, but dealing
pathetically with the humbler sort of people.
Of this irregular species Lillo's 'George Barn-
well' and Moore's 'Gamester' may serve as
specimens. Difficult to classify as these plays
may have been, they were moving in their appeal to the emotions of the London citizens; and
they must be accepted as spontaneous attempts
at a kind of play which the French later in the
century were to strive for under the name of
tragédie bourgeoise, the tragedy of common life,
with no vain tinsel of royalty and no false perspective of antiquity.

In France, where comedy and tragedy were
more rigorously restricted than in England, the
vogue of sentimental-comedy was less fleeting,
sustained as it was by the sudden success of the
pathetic plays of La Chaussée and by the ardent
proclamations of Diderot. With all his intelligence, Diderot failed to write a single good play
of his own; but he was swift to see that the
prescribed molds of tragedy and comedy, as the
French theorists had established them, were not
only too narrow but above all too few for a

proper representation of the infinite variety of human life. Envying the larger liberty of the English theater and approving of the *comédie larmoyante* and the *tragédie bourgeoise,* he demanded a frank recognition of the right of these new species not only to exist but also to be received as the equals of tragedy and comedy. Unfortunately Diderot could not sustain precept by example; his own attempts at play-writing were painfully unsatisfactory, and the tearful-comedies of La Chaussée were poor things at best, even tho they had won favor for a little while. Perhaps the most pleasing example of French sentimental-comedy was Sedaine's ' Philosophe sans le savoir ' ; and in spite of its amiable optimism and its touching situations, the tone of this innocent little play was thin, and its manner was rather argumentative than appealing.

IV

If we needed proof of the temporary popularity of the ingenuous domestic drama which pretended to be comedy, altho it preferred tears to laughter, we could find this in the fact that it tempted even Voltaire to essay it. Yet for sentimental-comedy it would seem as tho Voltaire had few natural qualifications, since he was deficient in sentiment, in pathos, and in humor.

274

Wit he had in profusion,—indeed, he was the arch-wit of the century; and he was so amazingly clever that when he attempted tragedy he was able to make his wit masquerade even as poetry. In the drama, as in almost every other department of literature, Voltaire is the dominating figure of his time. He was very fond of the theater, and he had possessed himself of some of the secrets of the dramaturgic art. He could devise an ingenious story; but he had no firm mastery of human motive. However artfully his plots might be put together, they were generally improbable in the main theme and arbitrary in the several episodes.

Even his best tragedy, 'Zaïre,' which is less of an improvisation than most of his other plays, and which still has an intermittent vitality on the French stage, was little more than a melodrama, as the characters existed solely for the situations by which they were created. Altho his versification was feeble, and altho he was never truly a poet, he was sometimes really eloquent. As a dramatist he was often self-conscious, not to say insincere; his mind was on the minor effects of the stage and not on the larger problems of the soul. His conception of tragedy was petty; it was without elevation or austerity; and yet he thought that the French had been able to improve on the type of tragedy which they had borrowed from the Greeks. He did not see that French tragedy, vaunting itself as absolutely Greek, had acquired from the Spanish drama a trick of complicating its plot with ingenious surprises, than which nothing could be more foreign to the large simplicity of the Athenian drama. He did not perceive that what his countrymen had been trained to expect and to admire in the tragic drama " was a set of circumstances peculiar to that play, with a set of characters common to all French plays in general, — the mesdames et seigneurs of the Spanish 'Cid' of Corneille, the Jewish 'Athalie' of Racine, and the Grecian 'Mérope' of Voltaire " himself.

How widely the ideal of tragedy upheld by the French dramatists under Louis XV differed from that pursued by the English playwrights under Elizabeth, and also from that followed by the Greek poets under Pericles, was made plain by Voltaire's own formal declaration in which he set up a standard of tragedy as he understood it: "To compact an illustrious and interesting event into the space of two or three hours; to make the characters appear only when they ought to come forth; never to leave the stage empty; to put together a plot as probable as it is attractive; to say nothing unnecessary; to instruct the mind and move the heart; to be always eloquent in verse and with the eloquence proper to each character represented; to speak one's tongue with the same purity as in the most chastened prose, without allowing the effort of riming to seem to hamper the thought; to permit no single line to be hard or obscure or declamatory; — these are the conditions which nowadays one insists upon in a tragedy." From this explicit definition it is evident that Voltaire regarded tragedy as a work of the intelligence rather than of the imagination; and it might even be inferred that he distrusted the imagination, and that he thought that the intelligence could be aided in the accomplishment of its task by the rules.

The rules of the theater, including that of the Three Unities, had been adopted in France in the seventeenth century largely because Corneille had given his adhesion to them, altho they held him in a bondage he could not but feel; and they were maintained in France in the eighteenth century very largely because of the authority of Voltaire, who was ever ready to reproach Corneille for every chance dereliction and to denounce Shakspere for every open disregard of dramatic decorum. The weight of Voltaire's authority was acknowledged not only in France but throughout Europe. His plays were translated and acted in the various languages of civilization; and his opinions about the theater were received with acquiescence in Italy, in Germany, and in England. It is true that in England, while the professed critics deplored the lamentable lack of taste shown by their rude forefathers, they themselves continued to enjoy the actual performance of the vigorous plays of the Elizabethan dramatists. It is true that in Italy the men-of-letters who accepted the rulings of Voltaire could take little more than an academic interest in the drama, since their theater was not flourishing, and even the comedy-of-masks seemed to be wearing itself out. It is true that in Germany also the theater was in a sorry condition, and that the German actors were often forced to perform in adaptations of French plays in default of native dramas worthy of consideration.

Charming as are certain of the comedies of Goldoni, they are slight in texture and superficial in character; and it is significant that Goldoni himself felt it advisable to leave his native land and to go to Paris to push his fortunes. Significant is it also of the increasing cosmopolitanism of the theater toward the end of the century that the plot of one of Goldoni's Italian comedies was utilized by Voltaire, whose French play was adapted into English by the elder Colman. Lofty as are the tragedies of Alfieri, they have a scholarly rigidity as if they were in-tended rather for the closet than the stage, altho the simplicity of their structure has made it possible to present them in the actual theater. Italy in the eighteenth century was sunk in corruption or busy with petty intrigue; and it was devoid of the energy of will which is the vital element of the drama. Not only was there little expectation or even hope of national unity: there was in fact but little solidarity of feeling among those who spoke the language. The French people, and the English also, were each of them conscious of their nationality and proud of it; but the Italians were like the Germans in having neither pride nor consciousness. Italy was only a geographical expression then; and no fervid lyrist had yet proclaimed the large limits of the German fatherland. The Italians and the Germans, whatever their merits as individuals, were then as peoples too infirm of purpose and too lax of will to be ripe for an out-flowering of the drama such as might follow hard upon the achievement of national unity and the establishment of a national capital. Very important indeed is the contribution which a city can make to the development of a dramatic literature; and not only Athens but also Madrid, London, and Paris have deserved well of all lovers of the drama.

V

ALTHO the Germans had then no center of national life and had not yet felt the need of it, they had given more proof of resolution than the Italians; and it was in the eighteenth century that Frederick laid the firm foundation of the national unity to be achieved more than a century later. It was in Germany again that there arose a stalwart antagonist to withstand Voltaire, to destroy the universal belief in the infallibility of French criticism, and to disestablish the pseudo-classicism which needed to be swept aside before a rebirth of the drama was possible. Lessing was the best equipped and the most broad-minded critic of esthetic theory who had come forward since Aristotle; and he had not a little of the great Greek's commingled keenness and common sense. The German critic was not so disinterested as Aristotle; indeed, what strikes us now as the sole defect of his stimulating study of the drama is its polemic tone. It was in the stress of a contemporary controversy that Lessing set forth eternal principles of dramatic art. He went into the arena with the zest of the trained athlete; and he was never afraid to try a fall with Voltaire himself. In fact, it was especially in the hope of a grapple with the French dictator of the republic of letters that the German kept his loins girded.

Lessing had not only a courage of his own: he had also the solid learning of his race. He was a scholar, thoroughly grounded and widely read. He knew at first hand the Greek drama and the Latin; he was acquainted with Shakspere and with Lope de Vega in the original; he was thoroughly familiar with the French theater, and with the criticisms made against it in Paris itself. Original as Lessing was, he profited by the suggestions of his predecessors, and there is no reason now to deny his immediate indebtedness to Diderot. The French critic it was who pointed out the path, but only the German critic was able to attain the goal. What Diderot had happened merely to indicate in passing, Lessing, with his wider knowledge of life, of literature, and of art, was able to accomplish. He took up the French rules of the theater with their insistence on the alleged Three Unities, and he was able to show the baselessness of the claim that they are derived from the practice or the precepts of the ancients. Then he went further and pointed out the inherent absurdity of these factitious restrictions and their fettering effect upon the French dramatic poet, even when they were kept only in letter and broken in spirit.

Lessing destroyed the superstitious reverence for the French theories; but he could build up as well as tear down. German literature was then at its feeblest period; and such original German pieces as might exist were almost as pitiful as the weak imitations of French tragedy. The German theater was battling for life; it was barren of plays worthy of good acting; it was almost as deficient in good actors capable of doing justice to a fine drama; and it attracted scant and uncultivated audiences without standards of comparison and therefore with little appreciation of either the dramaturgic art or the histrionic. Like Aristotle, Lessing had grasped the complex nature of the dramatic art, with the necessary correlations of playwright and player; and, like Aristotle again, he never thought of a drama as a work of pure literature but always as something intended to be performed by actors, in a theater, before an audience. The French imitations Lessing strove to eliminate by substitution,—by providing plays of his own which should be native to Germany in motive and in temper, and which might serve as the foundation for a national drama. He was almost as successful in this constructive effort as he had been in his destructive labors.

A critic Lessing was, no doubt, but a critic who had the rare ability to practise what he preached. In at least three plays he revealed himself as a true dramatist, as a man who had mastered the craft of play-making, and who could present on the stage the essential scenes of a struggle between contending forces embodied in vital characters. The proof of the play is in the acting always; and Lowell did not hesitate to assert that 'Minna von Barnhelm' and 'Emilia Galotti' act "better than anything of Goethe or Schiller." In justification of Lowell's assertion it may be noted that these two plays are nowadays seen in the German theaters quite as often as any two dramas of either Goethe or Schiller.

'Emilia Galotti' and 'Miss Sara Sampson' are tragedies of middle-class life, *tragédies bourgeoises*, owing something to the precept of Diderot and owing perhaps more to the practice of the English dramatists, whom Lessing had also admired. Altho his style is noble and direct, he is not primarily a poet, with the poet's instinctive happiness in finding the illuminative phrase. His culture, his formidable instruction, his resolute thinking, unite to give certain of his dramas a richness of texture uncommon enough in popular plays. 'Minna von Barnhelm' is a comedy, not tearful exactly, nor yet mirthful, rather cheerful, even if grave in spirit. Lessing was scarcely ever gay, altho he could be witty enough on occasion. His dialog has sometimes a Gallic ease, and it has always a Teutonic sincerity.

'Minna' is the best of his plays; it is brisk in action, lively in incident, and ingeniously contrived throughout.

Perhaps the model of which Lessing availed himself unconsciously when his serious plays were taking shape in his mind, was that suggested by Molière's larger and later comedies. But with his practicality and his perfect comprehension of the conditions of the modern theater, Lessing made one important modification in the form of drama which Molière had supplied. Where the Frenchman, dealing only with the crisis of Tartuffe's career in Orgon's house, had no difficulty in concentrating the action into a single day and a single spot, the German, rejecting the Unity of Time and the Unity of Place, held himself at liberty to protract the action over so long a period as he might find advisable, and to change the scene as often as he might see fit. But Lessing perceived the advantage of not distracting the attention of the audience by changes of scene during the progress of the act; and he therefore made his removals from place to place while the curtain was down. He was apparently the first playwright who gave to each act its own scenery, not to be changed until the fall of the curtain again. Here he supplied an example now followed by the most accomplished playwrights of the twentieth century

VI

In this avoiding of the confusion resulting from frequent shifting of the scenery before the eyes of the spectators, Lessing was more modern than either Goethe or Schiller, both of whom—especially in their earlier dramatic efforts, in the 'Goetz' of the one and in the 'Robbers' of the other—appeared to hold that the example of Shakspere warranted their returning to the more medieval practice of making as many changes of place as a loosely constructed plot might seem to require. Lowell suggested that there was " in the national character an insensibility to proportion " which would "account for the perpetual groping of German imaginative literature after some foreign mold in which to cast its thought or feeling, now trying a Louis Quatorze pattern, then something supposed to be Shaksperian, and at last going back to ancient Greece."

Nowadays Goethe's surpassing genius is everywhere acknowledged,—his comprehensive and insatiable curiosity, his searching interrogation of life, his power of self-expression in almost every department of literature. But great poet as he was, a theater-poet he was not. He was not a born playwright, seizing with unconscious certainty upon the necessary scenes, the *scènes à faire*, to bring out the conflict of will against will

285

which was the heart of his theme. He lacked
the instinctive perception of the exact effect likely
to be produced on the audience, and he was deficient in the intuitive knowledge of the best
method to appeal to the sympathies of the spectators. In fact, the time came in Goethe's career
as a dramatic poet when he refused to reckon
with the playgoers who might be present at the
performance of his plays,—an attitude inconceivable on the part of a true dramatist and as remote as possible from that taken by Sophocles,
by Shakspere, and by Molière. When he was
director of the theater in Weimar he did not hesitate to assert that "the public must be controlled." A more enlightened tyrant than Goethe
no theater could ever hope to have; and yet
little more than sterility and emptiness was the
net result of his theatrical dictatorship and of
his refusal to consider the native preferences of
the Weimar playgoers.

It was Victor Hugo who once declared that the
audience in a theater can be divided into three
classes,—the crowd which expects to see action,
women, who are best pleased with passion, and
thinkers, who are hoping to behold character.
The main body of playgoers has always wanted
to be amused by the spectacle of something hap-
pening before their eyes; and many of them,
including nearly all the women, desire to have

their sympathies excited; but it is only a chosen few who go to the theater seeking food for thought and ready, therefore, to welcome psychologic subtlety and philosophic profundity. The great dramatists have been able to satisfy the demands of all three classes; and 'Oedipus the King,' 'Hamlet,' and 'Tartuffe' were popular with the plain people from their first performance. But Goethe seemed to care for the approval of only the smallest class of the three; and only in 'Faust' did he reveal the dramaturgic skill needed to devise an action interesting enough in itself to bear whatever burden of philosophy he might wish to lay upon it.

Even in his early plays, in 'Goetz von Berlichingen,' for example, in which there is action enough and emotion also, there is no felicity of stagecraft. It purports only to be a chronicle-play; but altho afterward reshaped for the stage, it was not conceived to suit the conditions of the actual theater. 'Clavigo,' however, which is only a dramatized anecdote, an unpretending improvisation, swift in its action and clear in its handling of contending motives, is effective on the boards; and as a stage-play it is perhaps the most satisfactory of all Goethe's dramatic attempts, trifle as it is after all, devoid of either poetry or philosophy. 'Iphigenia' is a dramatic poem rather than a play; and 'Egmont' is little more than a novel in dialog. So fraternal a critic as Schiller confessed that he found 'Iphigenia' to be wanting in "the sensuous power, the life, the agitation, and everything which specifically belongs to a dramatic work." But if final proof is needed that Goethe, however various and powerful as a poet, was not a born playwright, it can be found, outside his own attempts at the dramatic form, in his alteration of 'Romeo and Juliet.' In this he not only modified and condensed both Mercutio and the Nurse, but he also substituted a tame narrative for Shakspere's skilful and spirited exposition by which the quarrel of the two families was brought bodily before our eyes.

VII

A THEATER-POET Schiller was, even if Goethe was not; yet Schiller's first drama, the 'Robbers,' was not written for performance,—altho it soon found its way to the stage-door, after the poet had somewhat restrained its boyish extravagance. Schiller rejected the model he could have found in Lessing's tragedies of middle-class life, a model too severe for the tumultuous turbulence of the storm-and-stress period. He followed Goethe, who, in 'Goetz,' had claimed the right to be formless as Shakspere was supposed to be. There is in the 'Robbers' a certain resemblance to the

crude Elizabethan tragedy-of-blood with its per-
fervid grandiloquence and its frequent assassina-
tion.

In this first play Schiller's stagecraft was
primitive and unworthy; he shifted his scenes
with wanton carelessness, and he let his absurd
villain turn himself inside out in interminable so-
liloquies. But however reckless the technic, the
play revealed Schiller's abundant possession of
genuine dramatic power. The conflict of contending passions was set before the spectator in
scenes full of fire and action. The antithesis of
Moor's two sons, one strenuously noble and the
other unspeakably vile, was rather forced, but it
was at least obvious even to the stupidest playgoer. The hero lacked common sense, no doubt;
but he had energy to spare; and at the end he
rose to tragic elevation in his willingness to ex-
piate his wrong-doing.

Dramatist as Schiller was by native gift, he
was but a novice in the theater when the 'Robbers' was written, and it was the fitting of that
play to the actual stage which drew his attention
to the inexorable conditions of theatrical performance. In his later dramas, in 'William Tell,'
for example, and in 'Mary Stuart,' the technic is
less elementary and more in accord with the
practice of the contemporary playhouse. But
Schiller appears to have been thinking rather of

his readers than of the spectators massed and expectant in the theater.   He seems to have taken
no keen interest in spying out the secrets of the
stage.   His plays are what they are by sheer dramatic power, and not by reason of any adroitness
of technic.   Indeed, in Schiller's day the German
theater was almost in chaos; and probably he
never saw a satisfactory performance of a dramatic masterpiece, German or French or English,
until he went to Weimar.

Despite his limitations, Schiller was the one
dramatic poet of the eighteenth century; he is to
be compared, not with Sophocles and Shakspere,
the supreme masters, but rather with Calderon
and Hugo.   He lacked their conscious control of
theatrical effect, but he had something of their
rhetorical luxuriance and their exuberant lyrism.
He was intellectually deeper than the Spaniard and
he was more masculine than the Frenchman.
Schiller's influence on the later development of the
drama would have been fuller if his structure
had been more modern and if he had profited
earlier by the example of Lessing, emulating the
great critic's certainty of artistic aim and imitating
his rigorous self-control.

But self-control was rarely a characteristic of
German poets in those days of impending cata-
clysm.   Lessing had emancipated his countrymen
from the tyranny of French taste, from the despot-

ism of pseudo-classicism. Other despotisms survived in Germany, not in literature but in life itself;
and a younger generation was ardent for the de-
struction of these survivals from the middle ages.
In Lessing's play the father of Emilia Galotti slew
his daughter to preserve her honor, while the evil
ruler who was responsible escaped scot-free. In
'Goetz' and in the 'Robbers' the aggrieved hero
was ready to turn outlaw on slight provocation,
and to revenge individual injuries on society at
large. The 'Robbers' especially had the super-
saturated sentimentality of the last half of the
eighteenth century; and it was filled with the
clamor of revolt, which was to reverberate louder
and louder throughout Europe until at last the
tocsin tolled in the streets of Paris and the French
Revolution was let loose to sweep away feudalism
forever.

VIII

The most of the German dramas of this period
of unrest were not intended for the actual theater,
altho many of them did manage to get themselves acted here and there. With all their wild
bombast and with all their overstrained emo-
tionalism, they were not without a significance
and a vitality of their own, a freshness of self-
expression wholly lacking on the German stage
before Lessing had inspired it. If these dramas

had been controlled by something of Lessing's self-restraint, if they had been less excessive in their violence, they might have afforded shelter for the growth of a dramatic literature native to the soil and national in spirit. But they were not healthy enough, and they soon fell into decay; and what did burgeon from their matted roots was the melodrama of Kotzebue, with its exaggeration of motive, its hollow affectation, and its tawdry pathos. Kotzebue's taste is dubious and his methods are now outworn; but his play-making gift is as undeniable as that of Heywood before him or that of Scribe after him. 'Misanthropy and Repentance,' known in English as the 'Stranger,' has caused as many tears to flow as 'A Woman Killed with Kindness'; and whereas Heywood's simply pathetic play was known to his contemporaries only in the land of its language, Kotzebue's turgid treatment of the same theme was performed in all the tongues of Europe, in Paris and London and New York as well as in Vienna and Berlin.

Melodrama bears much the same relation to tragedy and to the loftier type of serious play that farce does to pure comedy. When we can recall more readily what the persons of a play do than what they are, then the probability is that the piece if gay is a farce, and if grave a melo-drama. Even among the tragedies of the Greeks we can detect more than one drama which was melodramatic rather than truly tragic; and not a few of the powerful plays of the Elizabethans were essentially melodramas. So also were some of Corneille's, tho they masqueraded as tragedies and conformed to the rules of the pseudo-classics. Yet it was only in the eighteenth century that melodrama plainly differentiated itself from every other dramatic species.

The "tradesmen's tragedies" of Lillo and Moore in England and the tearful-comedies of La Chaussée and Sedaine in France had helped along its development; but it was Kotzebue in Germany who was able at last to reveal its large possibilities. In the pieces which the German playwright was prolific in bringing forth there was something exactly suited to the temper of the times; and this helped to make his vogue cosmopolitan. He was the earliest play-maker whose dramas were instantly plagiarized everywhere; and in this he was the predecessor of Scribe and Sardou. He influenced men like Lewis in England and like Pixérécourt and Ducange in France. In the works of the Parisian playwrights there was a deftness of touch not visible in the pieces of Kotzebue, who was heavy-handed; as Amiel once suggested, it is not unusual to see "the Germans heap the fagots for the pile, the French bring the fire." It was this French modification of eighteenth century German melodrama which was to serve as a model for French romanticist drama in the nineteenth century.

A century is only an artificial period of time adopted for the sake of convenience and corresponding to no logical division of literary history. None the less are we able to perceive in one century or in another certain marked characteristics. No doubt every century is more or less an era of transition; but surely the eighteenth century seems to deserve the description better than most. For nearly three quarters of its career, it appears to us prosaic in many of its aspects, dull and gray and uninteresting; but it was ever a battle-ground for contending theories of literature and of life. In the drama more especially it was able to behold the establishment and the disestablishment of pseudo-classicism.

At its beginning the influence of the French had won wide-spread acceptance for the rules with their insistence on the Three Unities and on the separation of the comic and the tragic. At its end every rule was being violated wantonly; and the drama itself seemed almost as lawless as the bandits it delighted in bringing on the stage so abundantly. Throughout Europe, except in France, the theater had broken its bonds; and even in France, the last stronghold of the theorists, freedom was to come early in the nineteenth century. Lessing had undermined the fortress of pseudo-classicism; and the walls of its last citadel were to fall with a crash at the first blast on the trumpet of Hernani.

IX. THE DRAMA IN THE NINETEENTH CENTURY

I

THE dawn of the nineteenth century was illumined by the last flickers of the red torch of the French Revolution; and its earlier years were filled with the reverberating cannonade of the Napoleonic conquests. It was not until after Waterloo that the battle-field of Europe became only a parade-ground; and this is perhaps one reason why there was a dearth of dramatic literature in the first quarter of the century and why no dramatist of prominence flourished,— excepting only the gentle Grillparzer far away in Vienna. In war-time the theaters are filled often enough, but the entertainment they proffer then is rarely worthy of the hour. Altho the drama must deal directly with a contest of human souls, it does not flourish while there is actual fighting absorbing the attention of the multitude; but when great captains and their drums depart, then are the stronger spirits again attracted to the stage.

Despite their survival in the Austrian theaters Grillparzer's pleasing plays are no one of them epoch-making; altho they had more life in them than the closet-dramas upon which British bards like Byron and Shelley were then misdirecting their efforts. Throughout Europe during the first score years of the century the acted drama was for the most part frankly unliterary and the so-called literary drama was plainly unactable, proving itself pitifully ineffective whenever it chanced to be put on the stage. In Germany the more popular plays were either sentimental or melodramatic; and sometimes they were both. In England the more serious dramas were frequently adapted or imitated from the German, while the comic plays — like those of the younger Colman — were often little better than helter-skelter patchworks of exaggerated incident and contorted caricature. In France tragedy was being strangled in the tightening bonds imposed by the classicist rules; and comedy was panting vainly for a larger freedom of theme and of treatment. But even in France help was at hand; and in certain Parisian theaters, wholly without literary pretensions, two species were growing to maturity, destined each of them to reinvigorate the more literary drama.

One species was the *comédie-vaudeville* of Scribe, with its attempt to enchain the interest of the spectator by an artfully increasing intricacy of plot; and the other was the melodrama of Pixérécourt and Ducange, derived more or less directly from the emotional drama of Kotzebue, but depending not so much on the depicting of passion as on the linking together of startling situations at once unexpected by the spectator and yet carefully prepared for by the playwright. 'Thirty Years of a Gambler's Life' is a typical example of this French melodrama, none the less typical that one of its most striking incidents had been borrowed from a German play. The *comédie-vaudeville* and the melodrama of the boulevard theaters were fortunately fettered by no rules, obeying only the one law, that they had to please the populace. They grew up spontaneously and abundantly; they were heedlessly unliterary; they were curbed by no criticism,— which was never wasted by the men-of-letters on these species of the drama, deemed quite beneath their notice.

The *comédie-vaudeville* of Scribe and the melodrama of Pixérécourt were alike in that they both were seeking success by improving the mere mechanism of play-making and in that they both were willing to sacrifice everything else to sheer ingenuity of structure. Unpretending as was each of the two species, its popularity was undeniable; it accomplished its purpose satisfactorily; and it needed only to be accepted by the men-of-letters and to be endowed with the literature it lacked.   Nothing is more striking in the history of the French drama of the first quarter of the century than the contrast between the sturdy vitality of these two unliterary species, *comédie-vaudeville* and melodrama, and the anemic lethargy of the more literary comedy and tragedy.   The fires of the Revolution had flamed up fiercely, and the French, having cast out the Ancient Régime, had remade the map of Europe regardless of vested rights; but in the theater they were still in the bonds of the pseudo-classicism which had been rejected everywhere else, even in Germany.   Comedy, as it was then composed by the adherents of the classicist theories, was thin and feeble, painfully trivial and elaborately wearisome; and tragedy, as the classicist poets continued to perpetrate it, was even more artificial and void.   In fact, so far as classicism was concerned, comedy was moribund and tragedy was defunct, even tho they neither of them suspected it.

Now, as we look back across the years, we cannot but wonder why the task of ousting the dying and the dead should have seemed so arduous or have caused so much commotion.   We marvel why there was need of a critical manifesto like Victor Hugo's preface to his 'Cromwell' or of a critical controversy over the difference between the Classic and the Romantic. Even then it ought to have been easily evident that there was nothing classic about the comedies and the tragedies which continued to be composed laboriously in accordance with the alleged rules of the theater; and even the defenders of the traditional faith might have suspected that there was really nothing sacrosanct about mere pseudo-classicism.

But few on either side could see clearly. The classicist deemed himself to be defending the holy cause of Art against a band of irreverent outlaws, striving to capture the temple of taste that they might debase the standards and defile the sanctuary. The romanticist swept forward recklessly to the assault, proclaiming that he had rediscovered Truth, which had been buried, and boasting that he was to revive Art, which had long lain asleep awaiting his arrival. Tho the defenders stood to their guns valiantly, and tho they asserted their intention of dying in the last ditch, they never had a chance against their superb besiegers,— ardent young fellows, all of them, sons of soldiers, begotten between two battles and cradled to the mellow notes of the bugle. For nearly twoscore years the French people had made a profuse expenditure of energy; and the time was ripe for a new birth of the French drama.

II

THE younger generation abhorred the artificiality and the emptiness of the plays presented at the Théâtre Français; and they were bitter in denouncing the absurdity of the rules. Like all literary reformers, they proclaimed a return to nature; and they asserted their right to represent life as they saw it, in its ignoble aspects as well as in its nobler manifestations. They claimed freedom to range through time and space at will, to mingle humor and pathos, to ally the grotesque with the terrible, and to take for a hero an outcast of the middle ages instead of a monarch of antiquity.

But a critical controversy like this with its spectacular interchange of hurtling epithets need have little effect upon the actual theater. Even in Paris the bulk of the playgoers cared little or nothing about the artistic precepts which a dramatist might accept or reject; it was only his practice that concerned them. If his plays seized their attention, holding them interested and releasing them satisfied that they had enjoyed the pleasure proper to the theater,— then his principles might be what he pleased. They neither knew nor cared what party he might belong to or what rules he might hold binding. And here the broad public showed its usual common sense, which prompts it ever to refuse to be amused by what it does not really find amusing. The playgoers as a body wanted in France early in the nineteenth century what they had wanted in Spain and in England early in the seventeenth century, — and what, indeed, the playgoers as a body want now in the twentieth century, what they always have wanted and what they always will want. What this is Victor Hugo has told us: they want, first of all, action; then they crave the display of passion to excite their sympathy; and finally they relish the depicting of human nature, to satisfy man's eternal curiosity about himself.

These wants the old fogies of pseudo-classicism did not understand, and this is why the public received with avidity the earlier plays of the romanticists with their abundant movement, their vivacity, their color, and their sustaining emotion. Alexander Dumas came first with 'Henri III et sa Cour'; Alfred de Vigny followed speedily with his spirited arrangement of 'Othello'; and at last Victor Hugo assured the triumph of the movement, when he brought out 'Hernani' with its picturesqueness of scenery, its constant succession of striking episodes, its boldly contrasted characters and its splendidly lyrical verse. Significant it is that Hugo and Dumas were both of them sons of Revolutionary generals, while Vigny was himself a soldier. Dumas increased the impression of his early play by producing the 'Tour de Nesle' and 'Antony,' marvels of play-making skill both of them, and surcharged with passion. Vigny won attention again with his delicate and plaintive 'Chatterton.' Hugo put forth a succession of plays in verse and in prose, all of them challenging admiration by qualities rarely united in a dramatist's work, and yet no one of them establishing itself in popular favor by the side of 'Hernani,' excepting only 'Ruy Blas.'

The flashing brilliancy of Hugo's versification blinded many spectators for a brief season and prevented most of them from seeing what was made plain at last only by an analysis of the plays in prose, 'Mary Tudor,' for example. When no gorgeously embroidered garment draped the meager skeleton it was not difficult to discover that Victor Hugo was not a great dramatic poet, "of the race and lineage of Shakspere." A great poet he was beyond all question, perhaps the greatest poet of the century; but his gift was lyric and not dramatic. He was a lyrist of incomparable vigor, variety, and sonority; and as a lyrist he had often an almost epic amplitude of vision. As a dramatist his outlook was narrow and petty; he could not conceive boldly a lofty theme, treating it with the unfailing simplicity of the masters. His subjects were lacking in nobility, in dignity, in stateliness. His plots were violent and extravagant; and his characters were as forced as his situations. The poetry to be found in his plays is external rather than internal; it is almost an afterthought. Under the lyrical drapery which is so deceptive at first, there is no more than a melodrama.

Melodrama for melodrama, 'Hernani' and 'Ruy Blas,' fascinating as they are, seem now to be less easily and less spontaneously devised than 'Antony' and the 'Tour de Nesle.' Dumas was a born playwright with an instinctive felicity in handling situation; and Hugo, altho he was able, by dint of hard work and by sheer cleverness, to make plays that could please in the theater, had far less of the native faculty. In their play-making both Hugo and Dumas were pupils of Pixérécourt and Ducange; and 'Hernani' and 'Antony' do not differ greatly in kind from 'Thirty Years of a Gambler's Life,' however superior they may be in power, in vitality, and, above all, in style. What Dumas and Hugo did was little more than to take the melodrama of the boulevard theaters and to make literature of it, — just as Marlowe had taken the unpretending but popular chronicle-play as the model of his 'Edward II.'

The French playwrights who supplied the stage of the boulevard theaters had borrowed from the German playwrights of the storm-and-stress a habit for choosing for a hero an outcast

or an outlaw. Here again they were followed
by the dramatists of the romanticist movement,
who were forever demanding sympathy for the
bandit and the bastard,— Hernani was the one
and Antony was the other. A note of revolt
rang through the French theater in the second
quarter of the century; a cry of protest against
the social order echoed from play to play. In
their reaction against the restrictions which the
classicists had insisted upon, the romanticists
went beyond liberty almost to license, and they
did not always stop short of licentiousness. They
posed as defenders of the rights of the individual
against the tyranny of custom, and thus they were
led to glorify a selfish and lawless egotism. There
was truth in the remark of a keen French critic that
the communism of 1871 was the logical successor
of the romanticism of 1830. To say this is to
suggest that the foundation of romanticism was
unsound and unstable. As a whole, romanticism
was destructive only; it had no strength for construction. When it had swept classicism aside
and cleared the ground, then its work was done,
and all that was left for it to do was itself to die.

III

Of all the manifold influences that united to
reinvigorate the drama toward the middle of the

century, the most powerful was that of prose-fiction. In France more particularly no stimulant was more potent than the series of realistic investigations into the conditions and the results of modern life which Balzac comprehensively entitled the 'Human Comedy.' The novel is the department of literature which was as characteristic of the nineteenth century as the drama was of the seventeenth; and only in the nineteenth was the novel able to establish its right to be considered as a worthy rival of the drama. Until after Scott had taken all Europe captive, the attitude of the novelist was as apologetic and deprecatory as the attitude of the playwright had been while Sidney was pouring forth his contempt for the acted drama of his own day. In the eighteenth century, when it ought to have been evident that the drama was no longer at its best, the tradition of its supremacy survived and it was still believed to be the sole field for the first ventures of ambitious authors. Men-of-letters as dissimilar as Johnson and Smollett, both of them hopelessly unfit for the theater, went up to London, each with a dull tragedy in his pocket. Steele and Fielding in England, like Lesage and Marivaux in France, were writers of plays to be performed on the stage, long before they condescended to be depicters of character for the mere reader by the fireside.

For years the novel was conceived almost in the manner of a play, with its characters talking and acting, projected forward and detached from their surroundings, as tho they were appearing upon an isolated platform, scant of scenery and bare of furniture. The personages of prose-fiction were not related to their environment nor were they shown as component parts of the multitude that peopled the rest of the world. Only after Rousseau had sent forth the 'New Héloïse' was there disclosed in fiction any alliance between nature and human nature; and only after Bernardin de Saint-Pierre had issued ' Paul and Virginia' did the story-teller begin to find his profit in the landscape and the weather, in sunsets and rainstorms and the mystery of the dawn, all phenomena not easily represented in the playhouse.

The novelist was long held to be inferior to the dramatist, and his pay was inferior also. But when by his resplendent improvisations Scott was able to settle with his creditors, the European men-of-letters were made aware that prose-fiction might be as profitable as play-writing. They knew already that it was far easier, since the technic of the novel seems liberty itself when contrasted with the rigid economy of the drama. The task appeared to be simpler and the immediate reward appeared to be larger, so that the temptation became irresistible for young men to adventure themselves in the narrative form rather than the dramatic. Yet not a few of those who took to fiction were naturally more qualified for success in the theater,—Dickens, for instance; and many of those who had won triumphs as playwrights sought also to receive the reward of the story-teller,—Hugo for one and the elder Dumas for another.

During the middle fifty years of the century it was only in French that the drama was able to hold its own as a department of literature; and in every other language it was speedily oversha-dowed by prose-fiction. Bold and powerful as the French novelists were, they had as competi-tors playwrights of an almost equal brilliancy, variety, and force. In French the drama and the prose-fiction were vigorous rivals for threescore years. But in German literature, in Italian and Spanish, the novel during this same period was at least the equal of the drama, whatever its own demerits; and in English literature the superiority of prose-fiction was overwhelming. In fact, dur-ing the second and third quarters of the century the acted play in English had rarely more than a remote connection with literature, whereas the novel was absorbing an undue proportion of the literary ability of the peoples speaking the language.

This immense expansion of prose-fiction, and

its incessant endeavor to avail itself of the devices
of all the other forms of literary art, will prove to
be, perhaps, the most salient fact in the history
of literature in the nineteenth century. But the
future historian will be able to see clearly that the
obscuring of the drama was temporary only, and
that even tho, outside of France, dramatic literature might seem to have gone into a decline, it
bade fair to be restored to health again in the final
quarter of the century. The historian will have to
indicate also the points of contact between the
novel and the play and to dwell on the constant
interaction of the one and the other,— an interaction as old as the origin of epic and tragic poetry.
It is to be seen in English, for example, in the
influence of the contemporary farces and melodramas of the London stage upon the incidents
of Dickens's serial tales.

It is to be seen in French also, of course; just
as Lesage and Fielding had applied to their narra-
tives the method of character-drawing which they
had borrowed from Molière, so Augier and the
younger Dumas were directed in their choice of
subject by the towering example of Balzac. The
Elizabethan playwrights had treated the Italian
story-tellers as storehouses of plots and motives,
of incidents and intrigues. But the Parisian dramatists of the Second Empire were under a deeper
debt to the great novelist who had been their

contemporary; it was to him that they owed, in a great measure, their quicker interest in the problems of society. They had not Balzac's piercing vision into the secrets of the heart, but they at least sought to face life from a point of view not unlike his.

IV

OBVIOUS as is the influence of Balzac upon Augier and the younger Dumas, especially in their later studies into social conditions, it is not more obvious or more powerful than the influence of Scribe. While the romanticists had been driving out the classicists, and exhausting themselves in the vain effort to establish their own sterile formulas, Scribe had gone on his own way, wholly unaffected by their theories or by their temporary vogue. He had been elaborating his technic until he was able to sustain the spacious framework of a five-act comedy by means of devices invented for use in the pettier *comédie-vaudeville*. In almost every department of the drama, including the librettos of grand opera and of *opéra-comique*, Scribe proved himself to be a consummate master of the art and mystery of play-making. He devoted himself to perfecting the mechanics of dramaturgy; and he has survived as the type of the playwright pure and simple, to be remembered by the side of Heywood and Kotzebue.

His plays, like so many of theirs, are now outworn and demoded. He is inferior to Kotzebue in affluent emotion and to Heywood in occasional pathos; but he is superior to both in sheer stagecraft. The hundred volumes of his collected writings may be consulted for proof that a play can serve its purpose in the theater and still have little relation to literature — and even less to life. His best play, whatever it may be, was a plot and nothing more, a story in action, so artfully articulated that it kept the spectators guessing until the final fall of the curtain, — and never caused them to think after they had left the theater.

Yet there were very few playwrights of the second half of the nineteenth century who had not been more or less influenced by Scribe, and who did not find it difficult to release themselves from their bondage to him. Even Augier and the younger Dumas, while the content of their social dramas was in some measure suggested to them by Balzac, went to Scribe for their form; and what now seems most old-fashioned in the 'Gendre de M. Poirier' and in the 'Demimonde' is a superingenuity in the handling of the intrigue. No small part of the wilful formlessness of the French drama in the final quarter of the century was due to the violence of the reaction against the methods of this master-mechanician of the modern theater. Even thoughtless playgoers began in time to weary of the "well-made" play, with its sole dependence on the artificial adroitness of its structure, with its stereotyped psychology, its minimum of passion, its humdrum morality, and its absence of veracity. But at the height of its popularity the "well-made" play was the model for most of the playwrights, not of France only but of the rest of Europe; and there was scarcely a modern language in which Scribe's pieces had not been translated and adapted, imitated and plagiarized.

It was in the second quarter of the century that Scribe attained the apex of success at the very hour when the romanticists were exuberantly triumphant; and it may sound like a paradox to suggest that it was the luxuriant abundance of the drama in French that helped to bring about its decline in the other languages; but this is no more than the truth. At the moment when the comparative facility of prose-fiction was alluring men-of-letters away from the theater, the dramatists outside of France had their already precarious reward suddenly diminished by the rivalry of cheap adaptations from the French. There was then neither international copyright nor international stageright; and French plays could be acted in English and in

German, in Italian and in Spanish, without the author's consent and without any payment to him.

As it happened, the French drama was then of a kind easily exportable and adaptable. The plays of the romanticists dealt with passion rather than with character; and emotion has universal currency. The "well-made" plays of Scribe and his numberless followers in France dealt with situations only; and their clockwork would strike just as well in London or New York as in Paris. The 'Tour de Nesle' and the 'Bataille de Dames' could be carried anywhere with little loss of effect. Few of the emotional plays or the mechanical comedies had any pronounced flavor of the soil; and they could be relished by Russian spectators as well as by Australian. But no foreigner can really appreciate a comedy wherein the author aims at a profound study of the society he sees all around him in his own country; and this is why the 'Femmes Savantes' of Molière and the 'Effrontés' of Augier are little known beyond the boundaries of the French language, while the 'Stranger' of Kotzebue and the 'Adrienne Lecouvreur' of Scribe have had their hour of popularity everywhere the wide world over.

So long as the theatrical managers of the German and Italian principalities, as well as those of Great Britain and the United States, could borrow a successful French play whenever they needed a novelty, without other payment than the cost of translation, they were naturally disinclined to proffer tempting remuneration for untried pieces by writers of their own tongue. This was an added reason why men-of-letters kept turning from the drama to prose-fiction, the rewards of which were just then becoming larger than ever before, as the boundless possibilities of serial publication were discovered, whereby the story-teller could get paid twice for one work.

V

WHEN we consider that novel-writing is not only easier than play-writing, but that the novelist had the advantage of a double market, while the dramatist was then forced to vend his wares in competition with stolen goods, we need not be surprised that the drama apparently went into a decline during the middle years of the century everywhere except in France. The theater might seem to flourish, but the stage was supplied chiefly with plays filched from the French and twisted into conformity with local conditions. As most of these hasty adaptations had no possible relation to the realities of life, there was no call for literary quality; and thus it was that there impended an unfortunate divorce between literature and the drama.

314

By the ill-advised action of certain English poets the breach between the stage and the men-of-letters was made to appear wider than it ought to have been. These poets fell victims to the heresy of the so-called closet-drama, which all who apprehend the true principles of the drama cannot but hold to be only *bon à mettre au cabinet,* as Molière phrased it. Averting their countenances from the actual theater of their own time, the English poets followed out Lamb's whimsical suggestion and tried to write for antiquity. Instead of letting the dead past bury its dead, Matthew Arnold and Swinburne put forth alleged dramas composed in painful imitation of the Greek plays, which had been originally planned in complete accord with all the circumstances of the actual theater of Dionysus. In like manner Tennyson and Browning spent their time in copying the formlessness of Shakspere's chronicle-plays, which were exactly suited to the conditions of the Elizabethan stage.

This writing of plays which were not intended to be played, and which had no relation to the expectations of contemporary spectators, was an aberration for which there is no warrant in the works of any truly dramatic poet. It was just as absurd for Tennyson to take as his model the semi-medieval form of Shakspere, regardless of all the changes in the circumstances of actual

315

performance in the theater, as it would have been for Shakspere himself to have slavishly followed the traditions of the Attic stage. It was still more absurd for Arnold to suppose that he could really get a Greek spirit into a play written by a British poet in the nineteenth century. Even if it had been possible for a man thus to step off his own shadow, there was nothing to be gained by venturing on a vain rivalry with the noble Greek dramas which have happily survived for our delight.

These unactable dramatic poems, with no bold collision of will to serve as a backbone, with scarcely any of the necessary scenes, without the actuality of the real play, intended to be performed by actors in a theater and before an audience,— these mistakes of judgment may have their importance in a history of English literature; but they need not even be mentioned in a history of English drama, any more than 'Samson Agonistes' will need to be mentioned there. Probably even those who most admire the poetry which has put on the garb of the drama without having possessed itself of the spirit are not sorry that Milton finally chose the epic form for 'Paradise Lost' rather than the dramatic. There is a taint of unreality about all these misguided efforts, whatever the genius of the authors themselves; there is a lack of vitality, due wholly to the fact that these

English poets scorned the actual theater. They yearned to reap the reward of the dramatic poet without taking the trouble to learn the trade of the playwright and without being willing to submit to the conditions he must perforce labor under.

Here Browning, for one, could have profited by the example of Hugo, who had perhaps no larger share of the native dramatic gift, but who put his mind to a mastery of the principles of the dramaturgic art, taking a model in the playhouse itself. The French had the double advantage over the English that their men-of-letters kept in contact with the actual theater, and also that the acknowledged masterpieces of their drama had been delayed until their stage had become almost modern in its lighting and in its use of scenery. Molière and Racine supply excellent examples from whose form there is no need to vary. Shakspere unfortunately planned his great plays for a stage still more or less medieval; and his masterpieces have to be modified and rearranged before they conform to the conditions of the modern theater. It was easy enough to borrow from him the loose framework of the chronicle-play; but it was impossible to steal the fire and force of his swifter and more compact tragedies. It is to be remarked also that we who speak English have rarely revealed the instinctive feeling for form which the French seem to have acquired through the Latin from the Greek. Quite significant of the French inherent regard for structural beauty is the fact that the gracefully lyric romantic-comedies of Alfred de Musset, published as closet-dramas, needed only slight readjustment to fit them for performance.

In the middle years of the century there was a living dramatic literature only in France. The romanticist drama had withered away, altho its spirit reappeared now and again, — for example we cannot help discovering in the heroine of 'Dame aux Camélias' of the younger Dumas a descendant of the heroine of the 'Antony' of the elder Dumas. But there is little flavor of romanticism in the best of the later dramatist's profounder studies of contemporary manners, — especially in his masterpiece, the 'Demi-monde,' which shares the foremost place in modern French comedy with the 'Gendre de M. Poirier' of Augier and Sandeau. The 'Froufrou' of Meilhac and Halévy was their sole triumph in the comedy which softens into pathos, while their lighter plays contained a fascinating collection of comic characters, as veracious as they were humorous. The comedy-farces of Labiche had not a little of the large laughter of Molière's less philosophic plays. The comedy-dramas of Sardou were the result of an attempt to combine the

contemporary satire of Beaumarchais with the
self-sufficient stagecraft of Scribe.

VI

BUT even in France the rivalry of the novel
made itself felt and its swelling vogue tempted
some writers of fiction to take an arrogant attitude and to assert that the drama had had its
day. Perhaps a portion of their distaste for the
acted play was owing to a healthy dislike for the
lingering artificialities of plot-making, visible even
in so independent and individual a playwright as
Augier and obviously inherited from Scribe. Yet
there was a still more active cause for their hos-
tility, due to their recognizing that the dramatic
art must always be more or less democratic and
that the dramatist cannot hold himself aloof from
the plain people. This necessity of pleasing the
public and reckoning with its likes and dislikes
was painful to writers who chose to think themselves aristocratic,— Théophile Gautier, for example, and the Goncourts.

One of the Goncourts was rash in risking the
opinion that the drama was no longer literature
and that in the existing conditions of the theater
nothing more could be hoped from it. Gautier
had earlier complained that the stage never
touched subjects until they had been worn thread-

bare, not only in the newspapers but in the novel. Here the poetic art-critic was making a reproach of that which is really an inexorable condition of the drama, so recognized ever since Aristotle,— that the playwright must broaden his appeal, that he cannot write only for the highly cultivated, that he must deal with the universal. The dramatist may be a little in advance of the mass of men, but it is not his duty to be a pioneer, since he can discuss the newest themes only at the risk of not interesting enough playgoers to fill the theater. If Goncourt had known literary history better, he might have remembered that the limitations of the theater had not prevented Sophocles and Shakspere and Molière from dealing with the deeper problems of life. If he had happened to care about what was going on outside of France he could have learned that even while he was recording his opinion, Ibsen was proving anew that there was no reason why a playwright should not do his own thinking.

The drama was not on its death-bed, as these aristocratic dilettants were hastily declaring; indeed, it was about to revive with new-born vigor, altho it was not to find the elixir of life in France. Since the Franco-German war there had been visible among the defeated a relaxing energy, a lassitude which French psychologists have regretted as both physical and moral. Whenever the national fiber is enfeebled the drama is likely to be weakened; and this is what took place in France in the final years of the century. Whenever a people displays sturdy resolution it is ripe for a growth of the drama; and this is what was to be seen in Germany in the two final decads when the French were losing their grip. Whenever a race, however few in number, stiffens its will to attain its common desires, the conditions are favorable for the appearance of the dramatist; and this is what had happened in Norway, where Ibsen was coming to a knowledge of his powers. With the appearance of Ibsen the supremacy of France was challenged successfully for the first time in the century. Ibsen's plays might be denounced and derided; but it was difficult to deny his strange power or his fecundating influence on the drama of every modern language.

Simultaneously with the natural reaction against the excessive vogue of prose-fiction and with the revived interest in the theater aroused by the occasional performances of Ibsen's stimulating plays, there was everywhere a revision of the local laws which had permitted the free stealing of French plays. An enlightened selfishness, an increasing recognition of the right of the laborer to his hire, and a growing sentiment of international solidarity led to such an extension of copyright and of stageright as to assure the dramatist the control of his own work not only in his own language but in almost every other. The playwrights of the rest of the world were relieved from the necessity of vending their wares in a market unsettled by an abundant offering of stolen goods; and they also received proper payment when their own works were translated into other languages to satisfy the increasingly cosmopolitan curiosity of playgoers throughout the world.

The new international laws even allowed the dramatist to reap a double reward by protecting his ownership of his play as a book also; and thus they encouraged him to seek the approbation of readers as well as of spectators. As a result of this wise legislation the pecuniary returns of the drama were raised again to an equality with those of prose-fiction, so that the writer who happened to be born with the dramatic gift was no longer tempted to turn novelist in despair of support by the theater.

The change in the law also brought with it another advantage, since the dramatist, having complete control of his own writings abroad as well as at home, soon insisted that they should be translated literally and not betrayed by a fantastic attempt at adaptation; and this tended to terminate the reign of unreality in the theater. So long as French plots were wrenched out of all veracity in the absurd effort to localize them in all the four quarters of the globe, even careless play-goers beholding these miserable perversions must have been struck by their "incurable falsity," as Matthew Arnold called it,—a falsity which tended to prevent people from taking the drama seriously or even from expecting it to deal truthfully with life. No artist is likely to give his best to a public which is in the habit of considering his art as insincere and as having no relation to the eternal verities, ethic as well as esthetic.

In the final decad of the century there was abundant evidence that the drama was rising rapidly in the esteem of thoughtful men and women. This higher repute was due in part, of course, to the respectful attention which was compelled by the weight and might of Ibsen's plays. It was due also to the efforts of younger dramatists in the various languages to grapple resolutely with the problems of life and to deal honestly with the facts of existence. Verga and Sudermann, Pinero and Echegaray, are names to be neglected by no one who wishes to understand the trend of modern thought. At the end of the century the drama might still be inferior to prose-fiction in English and in Spanish; but it was probably superior in German and in Italian. The theater was even beginning again to attract the poets; and Hauptmann and Rostand, D'Annunzio and Phillips, having mastered the methods of the modern stage, and having ascertained its limitations and its possibilities, proved that there need be no more talk of a divorce between poetry and the drama.

When the last year of the century drew to an end, the outlook for the drama was strangely unlike that of a quarter-century earlier. Except in France, there was everywhere evidence of reinvigoration; and even in France there were not lacking playwrights of promise, like Hervieu. Perhaps everywhere, except in Norway, it was promise rather than final performance which characterized the drama; and yet the actual performance of not a few of the dramatists of the half-dozen modern languages was already worthy of the most serious criticism. Just as a clever playwright so constructs the sequence of his scenes in the first act that the interest of expectancy is excited, so the nineteenth century — in so far as drama is concerned — dropped its curtain, leaving an interrogation-mark hanging in the air behind it.

X. THE FUTURE OF THE DRAMA

I

WHEN we stand upon the portal of a new century a glance back may serve to reassure us for a gaze forward; altho we must acknowledge that in the nineteenth century, as indeed in the eighteenth also, the drama did not pass through a splendid period of expansion such as made glorious its history in the seventeenth century. We are forced to remark that in the course of the last two hundred years the drama had lost its literary supremacy, partly as a result of its own enfeeblement, and partly in consequence of the overwhelming competition of prose-fiction, which was able to perform in the nineteenth century even more than it had promised in the eighteenth.

But we are encouraged to note that a score of years before the century drew to an end the novel was beginning to show signs of slackening energy, while the play was apparently again gathering strength for a sharper rivalry. In German and in

English, in Italian and in Spanish, young writers of ardent ambition were mastering the methods of the theater and were recognizing in the drama the form in which they could best express themselves and in which they could body forth most satisfactorily their own vision of life, with its trials, its ironies, and its problems. Even in French, in which language the drama had flourished most abundantly during the middle of the century only to languish a little toward the end, the final years were to be illumined by the triumphs of a young poet, possessed of a delightful fantasy and initiated into every secret of stagecraft. And afar in the Scandinavian land, which seems so remote to most of us, there still towered the stern figure of the powerful playwright whose stimulating influence had been felt in the dramatic literature of every modern language.

Thus we catch a glimpse of one of the most striking characteristics of the modern theater,—its extraordinary cosmopolitanism which made possible the performance of ' Cyrano de Bergerac' and of the 'Doll's Home' in every quarter of the globe. Not only can we find French and German plays acted frequently in New York, but we are glad to record that the English-speaking stage was again exporting its products, and that Mr. Bronson Howard's 'Saratoga' was performed in

Berlin, Mr. Gillette's 'Secret Service' in Paris, and Mr. Pinero's 'Second Mrs. Tanqueray' in Rome. Even more noteworthy is the fact that the playgoers of New York had been permitted to see an English play, 'Hamlet,' acted by a French company, a German play, 'Magda,' acted by an Italian company, and a Russian play, the 'Power of Darkness,' acted by a German company.

An educated man to-day is more than a native of his own country: he is also a citizen of the world, just as the educated man was in the middle ages when all Europe was governed by the Church of Rome and by the Holy Roman Empire, and when all men of learning wrote in Latin and studied the same Roman law. The spread of instruction, the ability to understand other languages than the native tongue, and the intelligent curiosity of the more cultivated public, have brought about a unity in modern literature like that which was visible in medieval literature before the Renascence came and before the population of Europe was segregated into separate peoples, hostile and intolerant. We have not let go the idea of nationality, and indeed we cherish it unceasingly; but we are not now afraid to see the idea of cosmopolitanism grafted on it.

In the middle ages the drama was almost the same everywhere; and a French mystery was always very like an English mystery, just as an

Italian sacred-representation was very similar to a Spanish sacramental-act. So at the beginning of the twentieth century the forms of the drama are almost identical throughout the civilized world. In structure there is little difference now-adays between an English play and a Spanish,— far less than there was when John Webster and Lope de Vega were almost simultaneously put-ting upon the stage the pitiful story of the sad Duchess of Malfi. There is a flavor of the soil about the 'Doll's Home,' about 'Magda,' and about the 'Second Mrs. Tanqueray'; the first is unmistakably Scandinavian, the second is indu-bitably Teutonic, and the third is frankly British; but in form there is little to distinguish them from one another,—just as there is nothing in the structure of any one of them to differentiate it from the 'Gendre de M. Poirier,' or from the 'Froufrou,' written in French during the same half-century.

II

THE cosmopolitanism of our civilization at the beginning of the twentieth century, the eager-ness of artists of every nationality to profit by what they can learn from their fellow-craftsmen in other capitals, the wide-spread international borrowing,— these are not the sole causes of the similarity of structure observable in the pieces of the chief living playwrights of to-day. There is another reason to be detected by extending our glance into the past history of the drama and piercing beyond the middle ages into antiquity. If we do this we cannot fail to see that this likeness of the English play and the German play to the French play is due in part to the fact that in all the modern languages the drama has reached an advanced period of its evolution, when it has definitely specialized itself and when it has been able to disentangle itself from the other and non-dramatic elements with which it was perforce commingled in the more primitive periods.

The history of the drama is the long record of the effort of the dramatist to get hold of the essentially dramatic and to cast out everything else. The essence of the drama is a representation of a human will exerting itself against an opposing force; and the playwright has ever been seeking the means of presenting his conflict without admixture of anything else. The tragedy of the Greeks, elaborated out of rustic song and dance, retained to the end the evidences of its origin, not only in the lyrics of the chorus but in their vocal music and in their sculpturesque attitudes. The drama of the Elizabethans, descended directly from the mysteries and moralities of the middle ages, was often prosily didactic, one character being permitted to discourse at undue

length, in much the same fashion as the medieval
expositor, and another being allowed to deliver a
bravura passage, lyric or rhetorical, not unlike the
tenor solo of Italian opera, frequently delightful
in itself but always undramatic.

The stage of the Elizabethan theater was
sometimes in the course of a single play made to
serve as a pulpit for a sermon, a platform for a
lecture, and a singing-gallery for a ballad; and it
would be easy enough to single out scores of
passages, even in Shakspere, which exist for their
own sake and which are not integral to the play
wherein they are embedded. But Shakspere could,
when he chose, anticipate the more modern
swiftness and singleness of purpose; and sometimes when he was inspired by his theme, as in
'Macbeth' and 'Othello,' he put all his strength
in the depicting of the central struggle which was
at the heart of his play. He excluded all accidental and adventitious superfluities, of which the
most of his fellow-playwrights never thought of
depriving themselves. There is also to be remarked in the Elizabethan plays generally a narrative freedom which is epic rather than dramatic. So in the plays written under Louis XIV
there is to be observed, more especially in Corneille's tragedies, an oratorical tendency, a prone-
ness to formal argument, which is equally aside
from the truly dramatic.

But this confusion is not peculiar to the drama
and it is to be studied in all the other arts also.
As M. Émile Faguet has put it clearly, "literatures always begin with works in which the
various species are either fused or confused, depending on the genius of the authors; they always continue with works in which the distinction of species is observed; and they always end
with works which embrace only the half or the
quarter or the tenth of a single species."   In other
words, there is always increasing differentiation;
there is an advance from the heterogeneous to
the homogeneous; and M. Faguet gives as a
typical example the simplification of Greek
comedy.   He asserts that the lyrical-burlesque
of Aristophanes was more or less a medley of
every possible species, — "true-comedy, farce,
pantomime, *opéra-bouffe*, ballet, fairy-spectacle,
political satire, literary satire"; and yet in the
course of less than a century, little by little, whatever did not belong strictly to pure comedy was
eliminated.   The chorus was cast aside, taking
with it the opera, the ballet, the fairy-spectacle:
and with the departure of the parabasis personal
satire went also, taking eloquence with it.   So
the lyrical-burlesque of Aristophanes was slowly
simplified into the comic drama of Menander,
which is but "the witty and delicate depicting
of average manners."   Latin comedy followed

Greek comedy slavishly; but French comedy, altho it inherited the classic traditions, still further differentiated itself into subspecies, Molière, for example, showing how pure comedy could sustain itself without the aid of farce.

The simplification of the primitive play, which was carelessly comprehensive in its scope, has been the result of a steadily increasing artistic sense. It is due chiefly to the growth of a critical temper which is no longer content to enjoy unthinkingly and which is educating itself to find pleasure in the purity of type. This more delicate appreciation of esthetic propriety is likely to be gratified only in the higher efforts of the dramatist, in those plays which plainly aspire to be judged also as literature. We need not look for anything of the sort in the more boisterous popular pieces which make no pretense to literary merit. In sensational melodrama, for example, we are none of us shocked by the commingling of farce and tragedy; and in operetta we are not even surprised by the admixture of lyric sentimentality and horse-play fun-making. But the more literary a play may be, the more elevated its quality, the more carefully we expect it to avoid incongruity and to conform to the type of its species.

It seems now as tho the unliterary plays, like melodramas and operettas, would always owe some portion of their popularity to sheer spectacle, to extraneous allurements devised to tickle the ears or to glut the eyes of the unthinking populace. But it is evident also that the critical spirit of the more cultivated playgoers is now inclined to resent the inclusion in the literary drama of anything foreign to the main theme, whether this extraneous matter is didactic or lyric, rhetorical or oratorical. They prefer that the stage should not be a platform or a pulpit. In Athens under Pericles, and in London under Elizabeth, the poets who wrote plays were addressing audiences which had not read the newspapers and which might welcome instruction nowadays needless. The impatient playgoers of our own time can see no reason why they also should not profit by the invention of printing; and they are quick to resent any digression from the straight path of the plot. They are frankly annoyed when the author ventures to halt the action that he may deliver a sermon, an oration, or a lecture, that he may declaim a descriptive report or an editorial article. They have not come to the theater to be instructed, but to be delighted by the specific pleasure that only the theater can give.

III

THIS elimination from our latter-day stage-plays of all the non-dramatic elements which are so abundant in the earlier periods of the drama has been accompanied, and indeed greatly aided, by certain striking changes in the physical conditions of performance, and, more especially, in the shape and size and circumstances of the theater itself. The modern playhouse is as unlike as possible, not only to the spacious Theater of Dionysus in Athens, with its many thousand spectators seated along the curving hillside, but also to the Globe Theater and its contemporary rivals in London and in Madrid, which were only unroofed court-yards.

The plays of Sophocles were performed out-doors, where the wind from the Aegean Sea might flutter the robes of the actors; and the plays of Shakspere and of Calderon were per-formed in buildings open to the sky, so that a sudden rain-storm might interfere sadly with the telling of the tale. The English and the Spanish playwrights were like the Greek in that they all had to depend on the daylight. The pieces of Molière were performed by candle-light in a weather-tight hall and on a stage decked with the actual scenery, which had been lacking in London and Madrid as well as in Athens; and this is one reason why Molière was able to per-fect the outward form of the modern play. The comedies of Sheridan and of Beaumarchais were produced originally in theaters externally similar to ours of to-day, but huge in size, villainously ill-lighted with oil-lamps, and having a stage the curve of which projected far beyond the proscenium-arch. It was on this space, beyond the curtain and close to the feeble footlights, that all the vital episodes of the play had to be acted, because it was only there that the expression of the actor's visage could be made visible to the spectators.

The most marked differences between our more modern playhouses at the beginning of the twentieth century and their predecessors a hundred years ago are due to the improvement in the methods of lighting, gas giving a far better light than oil, and the later electricity having many advantages over gas. As a result of the newer means of illumination the actor can now stand on whatever part of the stage it is best for him to place himself, and he is no longer forced to come down to the center of the footlights so that his features may be in the full glare of the "focus" (as it used to be termed). The footlights themselves are of less importance, since there are now "border-lights" and "bunch-lights," and since the whole stage can be flooded with a sudden glare or instantly plunged in darkness at the turn of a handle or two. The space that used to curve out into the auditorium has been cut back to the curtain; and the proscenium opening has now assumed the form of a picture-frame, within which the curtain rises and falls and before which no actor has any occasion to advance.

This change is far more momentous than it may seem at first sight — indeed, it is probable that its influence will be far-reaching. Only in the score or two years since the proscenium has become a picture-frame have all the audience been seated in front of the performers. Until then the acting had always taken place in a space more or less surrounded by the spectators and in closest proximity to them. In Greece the chorus and the three actors played their parts in the orchestra, around which the citizens sat in tiers that rose high on the sides of the hill. In England in the middle ages the performers may have presented the major portion of their mystery on the separate pageants, but not a little of the action was represented in the neutral ground around and between the pageants, and therefore in the midst of the assembled sight-seers; and in England, again, under Elizabeth, the stage was but a bare platform thrust out into the yard, with some of the spectators sitting along the edges of it and with the most of them standing on three sides. In France after the 'Cid' of Corneille and until after the 'Semiramis' of Voltaire a portion of the audience was also accommodated with seats on the stage. And in the eighteenth century, as we have seen, the stage curved forward into the auditorium far beyond the stage-boxes, the spectators in these being able to see the actors only in profile.

But in the eighteenth century the stage had been so far withdrawn that the use of the curtain became general to mark the division into acts. The absence of a curtain had forced Sophocles and Shakspere to end their pieces by withdrawing all the characters from the view of the spectators; and even Molière and Voltaire, perhaps in deference to the presence of those who sat on the stage, always marked the end of an act by a general exit of the performers. Not until the nineteenth century was well advanced did the dramatic poets begin to avail themselves of the advantages of "discovering" one or more characters in sight as the curtain rose, and of dropping it at the end of the act upon several characters grouped picturesquely.

The modern playhouse differs from its predecessors of past ages in the power to illuminate every part of the stage. Sometimes we are inclined to suppose that gorgeous spectacle, elaborate scenery, and ingenuity of mechanical effects are characteristics of our latter-day theaters only; but when we consider the records we soon find that this is not the fact. The late M. Nuitter, archivist of the Opéra in Paris (than whom there was no higher authority), once

337

assured me that there was no spectacular device
in which the Italians of the Renascence had not
anticipated the utmost endeavor of the moderns.
Leonardo and his followers foresaw all that could
be done in this direction; and they invented
many a marvel for the royal processions and for
the court-ballets with which their princes liked
to amuse themselves. It was in Italy that Inigo
Jones learned the secrets of the wonders he was
wont to display in the beautiful masques for
which Ben Jonson found fit words.

IV

THE Italian scene-painters and their apt pupils
in France and in England could accomplish all
that is within the reach of the most liberal of
modern managers,— excepting only the ability to
show the result of their labors properly illuminated. The power of directing at will whatever
light may be desired confers an advantage upon
the modern stage-manager denied to his predecessors; and it is certain to impress its mark upon
the drama of the next half-century,— just as
every other changing circumstance of the theater
in the past has necessarily registered itself in the
history of the dramatic literature that followed it.
What will hereafter be shown on the stage within
the picture-frame is likely to be increasingly pictorial and plastic.

338

The dramatist will profit by his ability to reach the soul through the eye as well as through the ear. He will be tempted to let gesture supplement speech, or even on occasion to let it serve as a substitute. In real life the action precedes the word; and it is sometimes so significant that the explanatory phrase which follows is not always needed. Lessing had seized this truth, which Diderot had half suggested; and he urged that the playwright should leave much to the player, since there were many effects which the actor could produce better than the poet. Herbert Spencer has remarked upon "the force with which simple ideas are communicated by signs"; and he noted that it was far more expressive to point to the door or to place the fingers on the lips than to say "Leave the room" or "Keep silent." The more accomplished the playwright chances to be, the more often he will have simple ideas to communicate forcibly; and the more frequently will he speak to the eye rather than to the ear.

In the ill-lighted theaters of old, the dramatic poet had to take care that his plot was made clear in words as well as in deeds; and he was tempted often to let his rhetoric run away with him. But in the well-lighted modern houses he can, if he chooses, let actions speak louder than words. Being able to reach the playgoers through their visual as well as their auditory sense, he sometimes plans to let a self-betraying movement do its work without any needless verbal elucidation. He recognizes that there are moments in life when a silence may be more eloquent than the silver sentences of any soliloquy. He is well aware that a sudden pause, a piercing glance, an abrupt change of expression, may convey to the spectator what is passing in the minds of the characters more directly than the most brilliant dialog. He has noted not only that emotion is often inarticulate when it is keenest, but also that a mental struggle at the very crisis of the story can often be made intelligible by visible acts; and he knows that the spectators are far more interested in what is done on the stage than in what is said.

At first sight it may seem to some as tho this utilization of the picture-frame must result in making the drama in the immediate future even less literary than it is to-day. This will surely appear to be the case to those who are accustomed to consider the drama as tho it was merely one of the divisions of literature, — or, indeed, as tho it was a department of poetry. But the drama, altho it has often a literary element of prime importance, does not lie wholly within the boundaries of literature; and it has always exercised its privilege of profiting by all the other arts, pictorial and plastic, epic, lyrical, and musi-

cal.   Above all, the drama is what it is because
of its specifically dramatic qualities; and these
qualities can be exhibited wholly without rhetorical assistance, as every one will admit who
has had the good fortune to see the 'Enfant
Prodigue.'   In fact, many a noble drama—
'Hamlet,' for one—has a pantomime for its
skeleton and calls on literature only to furnish
its flesh and blood.

The dramaturgic art being distinct from the
poetic, it can on occasion achieve results impossible to the lyric poet or the epic.   Indeed, its
ability to do this is the sole reason for its existence.   What need of it would there be if it was
no more than the echo of another art?   As Lessing asked with his customary directness: "Why
undergo the painful toil of the dramatic form?
Why build a theater, disguise men and women
in costumes, task their memories, pack all the
population in a playhouse, if my work, when
acted, can produce only a few of the effects which
could be produced by a good narrative read by
each at the fireside?"   And the younger Dumas
pointed out how an effect made in the theater is
sometimes so unlike any produced by a good
narrative read at the fireside that a spectator
seeking to recover, by means of the printed page,
the emotion that had stirred him as he saw the
piece performed, is sometimes "unable not only

to find the emotion again in the written words, but even to discover the place where it was. A word, a look, a gesture, a silence, a purely atmospheric combination, had held him spellbound."

But we may go further and insist that literature has a broader scope than is carelessly allowed it; and it is not lightly limited to mere rhetoric. It is not confined to phrase-making only. Literature goes deeper than style or even than poetry. It includes invention and construction; it is concerned with the meaning and with the propriety of the thought contained. It deals with philosophy and with psychology also. Now, if we take this larger interpretation of literature, we need not fear that the drama is likely to be less literary because the stage has receded behind a picture-frame. But it is likely to be less rhetorical, less oratorical, less lyric, less epic, more purely dramatic.

V

WHETHER it shall be less poetic also will depend not on any circumstance of the actual theater,— the use of a picture-frame, or the power of controlling the lights of the stage,—but on the attitude of the next generation toward the ideal. If the growth of the useful arts, if the advance of scientific discovery, if the spread of democracy, if any or all of these things shall tend to destroy our desire for the higher life,—if there is, as Mr. Leslie Stephen has asserted, "something in the very nature of modern progress essentially antagonistic to poetry and romance," then the drama of the future will be unpoetic, as all literature then must needs be. The drama will lack poetry just as every other form of art will be devoid of it, no more and no less. If, however, romance springs eternal in the human breast, if poetry is ever young, if beauty is born again with every springtime, if Mr. Stephen is wrong in his prophecy and if Lowell was right in believing that "while there is grace in grace, love in love, beauty in beauty, God will still send poets to find them and bear witness of them," —then the drama will have its full share of poetry in the future as in the past.

But we may venture the prediction that the poetry hereafter to be found in the drama will be less extraneous than it has often been hitherto. There may seem to be less of it, but what there is will belong absolutely to the theme. It will be internal and integral; it will not be external or merely affixed. It will reside rather in the conception of the story and in the relation of the several characters than in the language they may address to one another. The poetic playwrights of the future will be more likely to profit by the example set by Shakspere in 'Romeo and Juliet,' which is as beautiful in idea as it is in phrasing, than to follow that given in 'Measure for Measure,' the subject-matter of which is abhorrent, unworthy, and in itself unpoetic, however splendidly it has been draped in verse.

Such poetry as there may be in the dialog will be there, not for its own sake chiefly, but because it helps to enlighten the situation, to illustrate character, or to reveal motive. The action of the play will no longer pause for a rhetorical excursus like the satiric verses of Jaques about the seven ages of man. The set speech, the oratorical display, the *tirade*, as the French term it, will tend to disappear; and such lyrical passages as the poet may feel hereafter that he must have he will lead up to so artfully that they will seem to be useful to the story, just as Shakspere made Othello's description of his wooing, surcharged as it is with poetry, appear to be absolutely necessary to the proper presentation of the subject.

We can predict with almost equal certainty that poetry will not be wasted on unpoetical themes, as has happened only too often in earlier periods of the drama. The vivacity and the brilliancy of the verse in certain of Massinger's dramas, and even in a few of Beaumont and Fletcher's, should not blind us to the fact that the subjects are often sordid, and that some of these plays would have been solider pieces of work if they had been wrought in honest prose. This use of verse by the Elizabethan dramatic poets, even when the subjects they had selected were frankly prosaic, was unfortunately responsible for much of the unreality we can discover now and again in their plays. A beautiful theme may demand beautiful verse; but a tale of every-day life can best be told in the language of every day. Some of the Elizabethans seemed to find in blank-verse a warrant for an arbitrary disregard of the facts of life and for a freakish distortion of natural human motives. This is one reason why certain plays surviving from that glorious era lack plausibility and sometimes even sincerity. Fortunately prose has now established itself firmly as the fit medium for such plays as are not avowedly poetic in theme. Some dramatic poets at the beginning of the twentieth century are not ready to abandon prose even when they aspire to enter the realm of fantasy; and it has also been the medium chosen by M. Maeterlinck for his melodious dramatic poems, ever vague, often monotonous, and frequently formless, but at times rich in mystic beauty and in symbolic suggestion.

Prose, again, is what Ibsen has used in all his later social dramas, poetic and indeed almost allegorical as some of them have been in intention. Here we have another evidence of his profound artistic sense; for the fight Ibsen wished to wage prose was the best weapon,—a prose rhythmic, modulated, flexible, picked clean of all verbiage, and adjusting itself sinuously to the thought it had to express. A prose that achieved its purpose so perfectly had almost the beauty of poetry; and there was a like perfection in the structure of his plots, as masterly as they are straightforward.

The art of the drama, so an acute American critic has pointed out, is parallel to the art of the great builders " in the sequence of its parts, its ordered beauty, the inevitableness of its converging lines, its manifestation of superintending thought." In the dramaturgic art, as in the architectural, the latest form may be only a reversion to a primitive type newly adjusted with all the modern improvements; and as our towering steel-frame buildings are in fact only the humble frame-house of our forefathers wrought in metal instead of in timber, so the constructive methods of Ibsen are closely akin to those of Sophocles, however different the ancient play may be from the modern in subject-matter.

In the effort to grasp this severity of form, the playwrights of the twentieth century will be influenced also by the steadily increasing interest in personality. The lyric, which is ever the expression of an individual emotion, is now far more widely cultivated than any other species of poetry; and in prose-fiction there is an irresistible tendency toward a more careful and a more minute delineation of character.   In the drama, an intrigue of which the convolutions shall seem artificial or arbitrary will be incompatible with any depth of character-analysis.   The interest in personality is perhaps a chief cause of the insistence upon a strict adherence to the admitted facts of life, and of that relish for realism and for the subtleties of psychology which may be called the predominant characteristics of serious prose-fiction at the end of the nineteenth century.   It is probably also one of the springs of that desire to understand sympathetically members of other classes than our own, which is likely to exert an obvious influence upon the drama of the immediate future.

If the dramatist is to respond to this interest in personality, and if he is to reflect the social movement of his own age, then he will have an added reason for striving to deal boldly with his main theme, avoiding all complexity of plot-mongering, which is necessarily inconsistent with any sincerity of character-drawing.   He will acquaint himself with the methods of Scribe; but he will not allow himself to hold Scribe's theories too exclusively.   Scribe had adjusted situations so adroitly, one impinging on the other, that he had

347

no need of a serious study of men and women. Indeed, he had no room for anything of the sort; and in his workshop, as in so many others, machinery had ousted human beings. Then the younger Dumas, brought up in the play-factory of his father, was able to make the mechanism less intricate, and so to provide room for a little emotion and a little humanity. At last Ibsen, trained in the theater itself and familiar with every device of French stagecraft, made his profit out of all his predecessors and perfected a technic of his own, which represents that advanced condition of an art when the utmost ingenuity is utilized to avoid artificiality and when complexity is made to take on the appearance of simplicity.

Thus it is that Ibsen stretches back across the centuries to clasp hands with Sophocles; and a comparison of the sustaining skeleton of the story in 'Oedipus the King' with that in 'Ghosts' will bring out the fundamental likeness of the Scandinavian dramatist to the Greek,—at least in so far as the building of their plots is concerned. Inspired in the one case by the idea of fate and in the other by the doctrine of heredity, each of them worked out a theme of overwhelming import and of weighty simplicity. Each of them in his drama dealt not so much with action in the present before the eyes of the spectator, as with the appalling and inexorable consequences of action in the past before the play began. In both dramas these deeds done long ago are not set forth in a brief exposition more or less ingeniously included in the earlier scenes: they are slowly revealed one by one in the course of the play, and each at the moment when the revelation is most harrowing.

The influence of Ibsen has been felt in all the theaters of civilization, and none the less keenly by playwrights who would deny that they were his disciples, who dislike his attitude, and who disapprove of his subjects. His influence has been exerted both upon the manner of the contemporary drama and upon its matter. His technic is the last word of craftsmanship; yet it never flaunts its surpassing dexterity in the eyes of the playgoer, for it has the saving grace that its ingenuity is so abundant that it can conceal itself. And Ibsen has shown how this technic could be employed in the depicting of modern life with its inconsistencies, its reticences, its unwillingness to look into itself. His social plays—tragic, some of them, deep and searching always, yet sometimes freakish and unconvincing—stand as a complete answer to those who think that the drama is now only the idle amusement of men and women who are digesting their dinners.

An idle amusement the theater often is now, as it always has been in the past; and the stage is only too often occupied by empty spectacle. Yet the drama in its graver aspects, the drama as a contribution to literature and as a form of poetry, is not dead, nor is it dying. Indeed, there is evidence that it is on the threshold of a new youth. Signs of its refreshed vitality can be found by whoso cares to keep his eyes open and his mind free from prejudice. It bids fair to win back the attention of many who have been taken captive by the flexibility and freedom of prose-fiction. It cannot do all that the novel may accomplish; but it can do many things that the novel is striving vainly to achieve.

Only the future can decide whether or not the drama is successfully to contest the present supremacy of prose-fiction. Years may elapse before the play shall evict the novel from its apparent primacy; or it may never be able to resume its former superiority. The two most obvious characteristics of the century that has gone are the spread of democracy and the growth of the scientific spirit; and in the century that has just begun we may discover that the drama, which has always been democratic of necessity, shall prove also to be more satisfying than prose-fiction to a people bred to science. Even now we can see that not only the plays of Ibsen but also those of Björnson and Sudermann, of Verga and Echegaray, of Hervieu and Pinero, stand forward to show that the drama can deal adequately and suggestively with some of the problems of existence as these present themselves tumultuously to-day in our seething society.

NC
F
D

AU